KEA____

ON KINGS

GREAT LAKES

CHINOOK TACTICS

WAY BEYOND

THE BASICS

CAPTAIN DAN KEATING

TWO FISH PUBLISHING

Manufactured in the United States of America

ISBN 0-9774273-0-7

Interior design by Angie Messinger
Diagrams by Charles Huenink
Cover design by Josh Visser

To my Beloved wife, Mary. Friend. Companion. Soul Mate.
Life is a journey and there is no one I would rather share the joys and
sorrows with than you. We've been richly blessed with four precious gifts
from God, Rebecca, Ethan Daniel, Kate and little Chloe.

I can't wait to see what the road ahead has in store for us!

Maldive Islands

Contents

SECTION THREE
Tactics, Techniques and Strategies for Great Lakes Kings

Dan Keating is the most instinctive Big Water angler I've ever met. In my job as editor of Great Lakes Angler Magazine, I've been able to ride along with many top trollers, and there's no doubt that Dan is one of the top Big Water salmon anglers anywhere.

What sets Dan apart from the rest is how he fares consistently well without having the latest electronics, the newest rods and reels, the latest flashers and all the other bells and whistles. His stuff is all well-maintained, but much is stuff he's had for years. In other words, he's a lot like most of us salmon trollers when it comes to being equipped. *He* just knows how to find fish and put them in the boat better than most of us do. While he's always open to new ideas, he takes what he has and makes it all work.

I've had the pleasure of giving seminars and salmon clinics with Dan, and when it's his turn to talk, it's my turn to listen and learn, right along with the rest of the audience. Dan's presentations are in-depth and intricate, yet completely understandable, and the attendees always crowd around him after the show is over, asking more questions, thirsting for more knowledge. Dan has brought that same willingness to teach into the pages of this book.

In this book, Dan covers the little things, but he also talks a lot about the basic mentality that we must have for consistent success. He uses more than 30 years of experience as a Charter Captain and recreational fisherman to provide guidelines for finding fish—usually the most important part of any equation for success. Dan also breaks down techniques so that any angler can understand them. In short, Dan has created a book that will help anyone—beginner or longtime pro—catch more fish.

I think anyone who has ever looked at the big blue expanse of water

and felt at all intimidated will be able to read this book and hit the Big
Lakes with more confidence the next time out.

                Dave Mull
                Editor
                Great Lakes Angler Magazine

Let's face it. The Great Lakes provide some of the most challenging fishing for North American fishermen today. These waters have a wide variety of ecosystems, sub-surface geological variation, and subtle water nuances. The shear diversity of the waters we fish, and the sharp, seasonal weather fluctuations require anglers to employ a variety of tactics to locate and catch kings. Despite the variety found within the Great Lakes, the basic techniques to locate and catch kings are remarkably similar from one lake to the next.

Of all the species found in the Great Lakes, it is the mighty chinook that stirs the greatest excitement in many of us. I was nine years old when I made my first foray out onto the Big Water. I began chartering when I was 18. Since then, I have spent countless hours on the water hunting kings. For me, Great Lakes chinook fishing is a passion—I fish from the heart.

In the following pages it is my goal to share my 30-plus years of experience chasing trophy king salmon on the Great Lakes. While I have learned much from other anglers and the school of hard knocks, one of the greatest secrets I've learned over the years is to listen to the fish and the environment. With the advent of technology many anglers today make the mistake of ignoring their immediate surroundings. This approach is one-dimensional and neglects a very important source of data—the fish and their environment. When you make adjustments to your fishing program you need to be observant and listen to the fish, the weather, and the lake.

Repeatability is another quality of great salmon anglers. Learning to recognize winning patterns and then duplicate or re-create those patterns when confronted with similar conditions will lead you to more kings. You know, king fishing really is not that complicated. You don't have to reinvent the wheel every time you go fishing!

This book is a mix of practical and theoretical teaching. It is divided into three user-friendly sections:

The Hunt for Oncorhyuchus Tshawytscha.

Lure Selection and Integration for Great Lakes Kings.

Tactics, Techniques and Strategies for Great Lakes Kings.

Section One unpacks the hunt for kings. For many, the challenge of the hunt is the greatest challenge. Success begins with a solid understanding of your opponent, Mr. Chinook. The secrets of how to locate schools of big kings spring, summer, and fall are also unpacked.

In Section Two we will examine the ever-expanding world of lure selection. Lure selection is part of the larger process governing fishing success. Running the right lures helps, but running them properly, in the right location of the group dynamic, with the right delivery device, is equally important.

Section Three focuses on specific tactics, techniques and strategies used to catch kings under a variety of conditions. *Keating on Kings* is full of the little observations that can only be acquired from spending years and years on the water chasing Big Water Kings.

Catching kings is not complicated, but it is work. To consistently catch kings you need to do more than just dump a few lines in the water and randomly tool around the lake. This book will help you to systematically develop a game plan for your home waters.

Fishing is a game of decisions. Every time you put a line in the water, you will be confronted with a variety of choices. Believe it or not, how you respond to these choices has a tremendous bearing on your success. This book will help you to understand the decision making process and teach you how to make wise decisions on the water. If you understand all the options available, you will be able to react to the season, weather, and moods of the fish. You will be catching trophy kings all season long!

Captain Dan Keating
captaindan@bluehorizonsportfishing.net

The Hunt for Oncorhyuchus Tshawytscha

How to Locate Chinook Salmon Throughout the Season

The challenge of the hunt! Being able to locate kings is the first step to success.
—CAPTAIN DAN KEATING

Trophy kings are not found under every wave. First, you must understand the nature of your target. Then you must build a game plan, analyze the water and local conditions, make educated decisions and then . . . the fun begins!

CHAPTER 1

A Philosophy Of Locating Kings

Have you ever hunted Big Horn Sheep on a rocky mountain slope? When a hunter scans the rugged terrain he knows a variety of large animals such as mule deer, elk, coyotes, cougars and bears are scattered across the landscape. These animals, however abundant, are not the target species. The hunter must scan the mountainside and analyze the nooks and crannies of the landscape to determine *where* he has the best chance of locating the target species, a trophy Ram.

Trophy Rams are not found on every mountain. Likewise, trophy kings are not found under every wave. Your posture, as a fisherman, toward the lake, is similar to that of a hunter. When you gaze across the surface of the water, you know that chinook salmon are not evenly distributed across all areas. In fact, astute anglers know that most areas of the Lake will be void of kings. Seasoned anglers recognize that key areas will hold higher concentrations of kings. Wise anglers know how to locate these key areas and concentrate their fishing efforts on these locations.

A hunter will use tools, such as topographical charts, GPS and binoculars to analyze the mountainside and determine a route to follow. He will not walk the entire mountain, looking for a Ram, which could take weeks, or even months. Similarly, you don't want to aimlessly troll around. Yet, that's exactly how many people fish. They start somewhere off the pier heads and begin trolling, *hoping* a king intercepts their lure.

You will catch more kings if you learn how to analyze the water and make educated decisions on *where* kings should be located, *before* setting lines. Having a plan, i.e., a road map, will help you eliminate water without wasting valuable fishing time trolling in a barren desert.

When chasing king salmon on the Great Lakes, your ability to locate concentrations of kings is critical to success. Yes, you need the right lure, in the exact color at the right depth on the right delivery apparatus at the right speed, however, all of these variables are meaningless if there are no kings in the neighborhood. *Being able to locate kings is the first step to success.*

This may sound elementary, but I am amazed at how many people skip this step and go straight to rigging and trolling tactics. Truly great chinook anglers are hunters at heart. They realize that kings are a schooling fish and key locations will hold greater concentrations of large kings.

How do you determine *where* to begin fishing? Are kings equally distributed everywhere across a region? Or, are they only in a few spots? Are they close to the shore? On the bottom? Suspended in the middle of

A well-equipped boat hunts offshore waters in search of trophy kings.

nowhere? Are kings' homebodies, staying in a location for days or weeks at a time? Or do they randomly roam the Great Lakes never settling into any particular location?

The answer to these questions is not black and white. In reality the schooling and migration patterns of kings can look very different depending on the season, port of departure, local weather and yearly patterns. Frequently you will find small schools or pockets of kings spread over vast areas off your homeport. At other times, kings will be widely scattered with few sizable concentrations. And then there will be days when kings will be tightly schooled in only one or two locations off your homeport. Regardless of the density of the king population or particular schooling patterns, chinooks are attracted to certain locations year after year.

Trolling is frequently a process of eliminating unproductive water. The Great Lakes are huge and kings are a far roaming fish. Every time you head out on your boat, you face massive amounts of open water. If you learn to eliminate water first, you will dial into productive locations quicker. A systematic methodology will lead you to more kings, help you to track fish movements and allow you to gain a deeper understanding of the regions you fish.

Building a Foundation:
Five Characteristics of King Salmon

If you want to consistently locate schools of large kings, you need to understand the nature of the beast. A solid understanding of the physiological character of your target is paramount to success. If you understand how your target behaves, you will learn to anticipate and follow their daily movements. You will be equipped to react to weather changes and you will be prepared to follow fish throughout the day. This understanding should have a profound impact on how you approach the water.

Before setting the first line you have to ask, *Who is Mr. King Salmon?*

What does he like to eat? Where is he most comfortable? How does he spend his spare time? Who does he like to spend his time with? The basic physiological tenants that govern the daily movements and bodily functions of Mr. King Salmon are crucial to success because they will lead you straight to your target. These character traits should form the foundation of your hunt.

King Salmon Are an Aggressive Predator

Great Lakes chinooks are at the top of the food chain. They are the kings. You don't get to the top of the food chain by being passive. Their aggressive nature will be a key component in helping you build a highly productive game plan.

Large kings require more food each day to sustain their bodily functions than smaller kings. Survival depends on their ability to locate and consume protein rich baitfish. In other words, kings need to eat a lot of baitfish to thrive. What is Captain Dan saying? Big fish, which need lots of little fish, will always be found near the bait!

As chinooks mature in their final year of life, their appetite increases as they pack on weight in anticipation of the fall spawning runs. Physiologically, their bodies are building up mass to carry them through the spawning ordeal. Remember, Great Lakes kings are Pacific salmon. Pacific salmon are genetically programmed. In their native West Coast setting, kings migrate across hundreds of miles of open-ocean before entering West Coast Rivers to spawn. In their indigenous setting, some strains of kings will migrate 100 to over 1,000 miles up coastal rivers! These fish are no longer feeding, but they are living off the proteins stored in their bodies.

If you take a moment to think about this, the life cycle of salmon is an incredible system. In their native Pacific coast setting, salmon harness the abundant protein of the open ocean. After feeding in the fertile Pacific, adult fish, fueled by the ocean, migrate up coastal rivers. After spawning, adult fish die and their carcasses decompose many miles inland from the sea. Their spent bodies not only feed animals along the river, but their decomposing bodies feed the bottom end of the food chain with nutrients brought in from the open seas.

In preparation for spawning migrations, kings feed heavily during their final months of life. Great Lakes kings do not have to travel hundreds of miles up rivers to spawn but the fish are not cognitively aware of that. They are genetically programmed to pack on the calories during the final stage of life in anticipation of a monumental migration inland. This is a good thing for anglers as feeding fish are easier to catch than dormant fish. I am a better fisherman when I am fishing around aggressive, feeding fish.

Kings Like Ice-Cold Water

In fact, large kings prefer much colder water than the other salmonids found in the Great Lakes. I believe 42 to 44-degree water is the peak range for catching big kings. Some may dispute but some of the biggest names in Great Lakes fishing, including former New York State Head of Fisheries Ernie Lantiegne on eastern Lake Ontario and Lake Michigan's Dynamic Duo, Dave Engel and Bill Best of Best Chance Charters, believe kings thrive in 42 to 44-degree water!

The primary strike zone for trophy kings is this thin layer of ice cold, 42 to 44-degree water. A secondary strike zone extends up to the 48-degree band. A third strike zone extends all the way up to the 54-degree layer. In subsequent chapters I will discuss the times of day and conditions that kings will be found cruising other temperature layers. I will also discuss how to fish multiple layers based on water temperature.

As you develop a philosophy of hunting kings, you need to incorporate cold water into your thought process. Water temperature is the key component to help you eliminate unproductive water. Yes, we've all heard the stories of catching a load of kings in warm water, BUT the majority of kings spend their time in icy cold water. You will spend more time under the pressure of bent rods and screaming drags if you pull your baits through water where kings live.

Bottom Topography Attracts Kings

Chinooks are a true pelagic species. They are highly migratory and can cover great distances. Kings that have been transplanted to our Inland Seas are Pelagic, but, since they spend much of their time in the lower layers of the water column, many fish relate heavily to irregularities in the lake bottom. Structure also appeals to kings because it impacts bottom currents and attracts baitfish. Savvy anglers know that key bottom features function like road signs—they lead you to fish.

Great Lakes kings frequently orient their movements based on bottom structure. In some regions of the Great Lakes, this very well may be the key factor guiding you to fish. How to use bottom structure to locate kings will be examined in the following pages.

Currents Impact the Migration Patterns of Kings

Current is really a bi-factor of the weather, bottom structure and the earth's rotation. Water currents are one of the least understood elements in Great Lakes fishing; however, they have a huge bearing on bait and predator locations in the Great Lakes.

The Great Lakes are unique. In terms of volume, they are huge, and share some similarities with the ocean. They are also landlocked and retain many of the attributes of inland waters. How water

Being able to locate kings is the first step to success.

moves is unique in the Great Lakes. Having an understanding of how masses of water move off your favorite port will help you locate kings before you even leave the harbor. If you understand how winds steer currents and bottom topography deflects them, you will catch more kings. You will think on your feet and react to fast changing conditions that shut most salmon anglers down!

Kings Are a Schooling Fish

Kings are not a solitary fish. When you find one, chances are he is not traveling alone. I am amazed at how many Great Lakes anglers view kings as a bonus fish. They go out, catch a bunch of coho or trout, then happen upon a king or two and that makes their day. Chances are, there are sizable populations of kings in your region that go un-fished much of the year.

Like many Pelagic species, kings frequently school by size. If you are looking for big kings, you may have to ignore schools of smaller fish and continue hunting. If I catch a big king, I will work the immediate area since large kings can be expected. If I go through a location and only catch 7 to 12 pound kings, I may elect to keep hunting for a school of larger kings. This size oriented schooling pattern is true all season across all the Lakes.

These five points should be incorporated into every fishing trip. If you understand these character traits and build your game plan around them, then you will be well on your way to catching more and larger kings.

KING SALMON MOVEMENTS: CAPTAIN DAN'S TWO-SCHOOL THEORY

What makes a king salmon swim from 40 feet of water out to 150 feet of water? What makes a fish move from a nice, bright location in the water column down to the dark, bottom layers of the lake? What leads one fish to migrate to the northern end of a lake, and yet another fish stays in the southern basin of the same lake?

When I look out the window at the world, I try to understand what I see and experience. When I look at the Lake, it is no different. I have been catching king salmon since the early 1970's and have been chartering full time since the early '80's. Many seasons found me on the water all day, just about every day of the week. During my time on the water, I've spent a great deal of time trying to make sense of kings and their movements and behavior.

Chinooks behave very differently than other salmonids. If you could classify daily movements of Great Lakes kings from a macro perspective, what would it look like? Based on the behavior of kings, I believe we can divide them into two groups or "schools." I call this the *Two School Theory*. To some, this may sound like an over-simplification, however, I am not writing a biological treatise. I am trying to help you understand the basic movements of kings so you can locate and catch more fish!

Now by "Two School Theory," I don't mean that there are literally "2" individual schools of chinooks in the Lakes, one off the northeast side of Chicago and the other school is off Buffalo. What I am suggesting is Great Lakes kings tend to follow two very different but specific patterns. Their daily movements will be governed by one of these two patterns. As you think about looking for fish, I want you to visualize the movements of kings from this macro perspective. This will sharpen and focus your fish finding skills.

The two schools are called:

1. Bottom Oriented, Near Shore Kings.
2. Open Water Nomads.

These two very different groups of fish are distinguished by their behavior. The near shore kings relate their daily movements to bottom topography. They will frequently be found in the bottom 10-20 feet of the water column. This group of fish will typically be found closer to shore. They spend most of their time in 60 to 140 feet of water. Their movements and location are closely tied to drop-offs, humps, rock piles and reefs and depressions in the bottom. When near shore kings takes up residence off a particular bottom structure, they often hold in that location for a week or longer. The same bottom structures will attract and hold kings year after year. Wise anglers keep a log of such locations and match local weather conditions and season to the GPS numbers marking these king magnets.

When conditions, such as water temperature or bait migrations change, near shore kings will typically move parallel to the shoreline rather than perpendicularly to the shoreline. They appear to tolerate warmer water temperatures and will frequently stay in the 60 to 140 foot range even when water temperatures elevate beyond their comfort zone of 42 to 48 degrees. These kings will stay in a region with bottom temperatures as high as 58 to 60 degrees, often holding close to the bottom in the absolute coolest water. These fish will hug the bottom during daylight hours. Typically, you will not mark them on your sonar when they retreat to the bottom, but they are very catchable.

The second group, the *Open Water Nomads*, will roam the deep, open waters of our Great Lakes. These fish are true Pelagics! Their movements will often appear random, hence the term, *Open Water Nomads*. Finding this group of fish is simply a matter of hunting. Open water kings will suspend in the water column from 40 to 200 feet down. At times, you will find them much deeper. You may encounter them in 180 feet of water today and 320 feet tomorrow. Open water kings will frequently move perpendicular to the shoreline when following baitfish and water temperature. I also believe this group of fish can migrate many miles in a single day.

Are the fishing patterns and techniques the same for both schools of kings? No. Open water kings are typically easier to catch than their nearshore brethren. Open water nomads will hit aggressively throughout the day. The nomads appear to move around more than the shallow water kings and hence, may be burning more calories. Theoretically, this would require them to consume more food to sustain their bodily functions, resulting in their being easier to catch throughout the day.

In a typical year, you will encounter both scenarios (fish from each group). In many locations, you will find different schools of fish following each of these patterns. Large, mature kings can be found in both the near-shore group and the open water nomadic group. Greater concentrations of juvenile kings (3 to 15 pounds) are usually found in the offshore realms.

Identifying which school or group of kings is dominant on any given day is critical. By identifying the target group, you will know where to begin your search and you can anticipate the fish's movements when conditions change. If near shore kings are dominating your local fishing patterns, then you should focus your midday fishing effort on bottom-oriented kings. Rather than drifting offshore, you may want to finesse fish off the bottom in the 70 to 140 foot range. You will want to move parallel to the shoreline looking for fish. If nomadic kings are dominant in the region, then you may want to concentrate on hunting deep water for mid day action. You will work perpendicular to the shoreline, heading offshore, as you look for kings.

Are near shore, bottom oriented kings the same fish as the open water nomads? Technically, yes. But from the angler's perspective, they

Captain Dan with Rebecca and Ethan, two of his favorite fishing partners.

are two very different animals because they require different techniques to catch them. As a king changes locations in the water column, vertically and horizontally, their behavior changes. A king suspended 70 feet down over 190 feet of water behaves very differently than a king sitting on the bottom in 60 feet of water. A king running the shoreline in 20 feet behaves differently yet.

This has major implications to the angler because the techniques required to catch a deepwater king are different than those employed in shallow water. Near shore kings are easier to catch at first and last light. Catching near shore kings during the mid-day requires a great deal of finesse. Lures that draw strikes 90 feet down are different than lures that work 30 feet down. These tactical differences are addressed throughout the following pages of this book.

BUILDING A GAME PLAN:
THE MECHANICS OF LOCATING KINGS

It's 5:30 a.m., and you've just cleared the pier heads, where do you go? How far offshore do you run before you start fishing? Do you go left? Do you go right? (I promise, I will not digress into politics here) How deep is the water where you should begin fishing? What pattern governs your line sets? What do you do if you set up in a desert? Do you change location? Maybe move offshore? Or, should you move parallel to the shoreline?

To help you zero in on the big concentrations of kings, focus on four critical elements: water temperature, bait fish, bottom structure and currents. The intersection of these four elements will frequently hold peak numbers of catchable kings.

Every time you make a decision on *where* to fish, go back to the basics. Remember the five character traits listed above? Those traits greatly influence daily king movements. They should also influence your fishing strategies and trolling locations, as they are the key markers leading you to schools of kings.

Let's roll up our sleeves and get down to business! How do you locate kings? Finding kings is like hunting and often it is a matter of eliminating water. Like many aspects of Great Lakes fishing, seasonal variations dictate much of what we do. For this reason, I will divide this discussion into three parts: Spring, Summer and Fall. There will be some overlap so I will try not to be redundant.

Understanding the basic characteristics of kings will lead you to catches like this.

CHAPTER 2

With Cold Water Everywhere, How Do You Find Spring Kings?

Spring across the Great Lakes region is as varied as a crowd at New York's Times Square. In some locations, spring begins in mid March. In other regions, snowdrifts inhabit the landscape deep into April. The spring chinook fishery on the Great Lakes is as diverse as the weather. In some areas, it doesn't exist. In other areas, it is short lived like a fourth of July fireworks celebration and in some regions, such as southern Lake Michigan and the western basin of Lake Ontario, the spring fishery is rockin'!

THE CHALLENGE OF THE SPRING HUNT

Historically, many anglers mistakenly believe you can only catch kings during the summer and fall months. These anglers are missing out on some great action as kings can be caught throughout the season. The key to catching kings during the spring is location.

Finding spring kings is challenging because the Great Lakes have not yet stratified. During the summer a thermocline sets up and schools of kings are forced down in the water column. Water stratification helps anglers eliminate vast chunks of real estate simply because much of the water is too warm for kings.

In spring the entire water column is ice-cold. Whether you are in 50 feet or 300 feet of water, 39 to 47-degree water will dominate the entire water column. This complicates your task as kings can find comfortable water anywhere. They may be in 30 feet of water, dining on a juicy alewife, or basking in 200 feet of water, enjoying the brisk chill of a May morning. Spring kings are fat and happy and roam the Great Lakes like a herd of cows grazing across the heartland of America.

With water stratification offering little help, how do you zero in on concentrations of spring kings? One approach during spring is to randomly troll across vast stretches of open water, hoping to stumble across a school of kings. Or, you can bring intentionality to your game by focusing on bottom structure and baitfish. During the spring large kings often relate to subtleties in bottom contour. Off my homeport in southwestern Lake Michigan, drop-offs, hills, ledges, humps, rocky reefs and depressions in the 50 to 120 foot range are ideal areas to probe. Top king anglers from other regions of the Great Lakes (Lakes Ontario, Huron and Michigan) tell me that they encounter similar situations on their home waters.

BOTTOM STRUCTURE LEADS TO KINGS

Ancient geological forces carved out the Great Lakes many years ago. If you could walk across the various Lake bottoms, you would find a wide variety of topographical variations. Since we cannot view these features, we need to rely on electronics and topo charts to illumine the way.

One of the dominant structure forms is drop-offs. Drop-offs that attract spring kings may be slight, varying only two to five feet or they may be more extreme. The degree or rate of *drop* is a variable determined by the ancient glaciers that carved out the Great Lakes. In some locations the drop-offs will be steep and a 20-foot vertical drop-off will occur over a horizontal distance of 100 feet. In other regions a 20-foot drop-off will cover a horizontal distance of half a mile. Both types of drop-offs could be king magnets during the spring months.

Smaller drops and humps are some of the most productive locations

WITH COLD WATER EVERYWHERE, HOW DO YOU FIND SPRING KINGS?   **19**

for spring kings. Off my home harbor, Winthrop Harbor, I fish a series of small drop-offs and humps that vary by 2 to 10 feet from the surrounding bottom. These structures are located between 40 to 140 feet of water. Most other anglers are not even aware of them! But these little jewels are my secret go-to spots for spring kings. The charter fleet will troll over these small drops and catch coho, completely oblivious to the big kings that are lurking beneath their spreads of coho rigs. When I troll over these locations, I drop baits to the bottom, and guess what? I catch big kings time after time off these minor features. If you don't pay attention to your bottom machine, you will miss these kings!

How do you locate these spring king magnets along the bottom? Larger drops and hills will show up on navigation charts. The smaller features, which are often the most productive, will not be noticeable on charts. The way to discover these honey holes is by close observation of your bottom machine. When you are trolling or running, pay attention to the graph. When you notice irregularities in the bottom, make note of them and study the shape of the structure. When you hook up with a king, watch the graph closely and look for structure. If you notice a slight irregularity in the bottom, make multiple passes over the location from a variety of angles to mentally map out the feature.

When searching for spring kings around bottom structure, look for kings suspended in the bottom half of the water column or holding tight to the bottom. Typically, your biggest spring kings will be found holding tight to the bottom, especially in the middle of the day. These are fish you rarely see with your electronics. When targeting spring kings in less than 120 feet of water I usually keep one rig, a downrigger with a clean spoon stretched 15 to 40 feet behind the ball, running within 2 to 20 feet of the bottom. The details of how to *trace the bottom* with a clean spoon are discussed in Chapter 8.

Fishing the Spot-On-the-Spot

When working bottom structure, salmon anglers can borrow a play card from our walleye and bass Brethren. These anglers key their efforts on the *spot-on-the-spot*. In other words, look for the smaller features on the larger pieces of structure. These nooks and crannies will frequently hold concentrations of larger fish.

The nuances I am talking about could be a sudden variation in the angle of the drop-off, it may be a little rockpile, a change in bottom composition or it may be a trench or, depression that runs through a flat area of lake bottom. For example, lets say a drop-off is running at a 20-degree angle and sharply changes to a 35-degree angle. Right where the angle changes is a good place to look for kings. These *corners* will attract baitfish and deflect bottom currents. On major drop-offs that run parallel to the shoreline, you will also frequently encounter a short section that drops quicker (vertically) than the surrounding drop-off. For example, a ridge or hill dropping off from 50 to 80 feet occurs over a half-mile distance. In a one-quarter mile stretch, the same drop covers a distance of a tenth of a mile. These small sections are gold mines! Areas of hard or rocky bottom surrounded by muck or clay bottom also attract spring kings.

Although it is more difficult for salmon anglers to locate these microstructures when fishing over 60 to 140 feet of water than a bass angler working a ridge in 12 feet of water, it is not impossible. Savvy

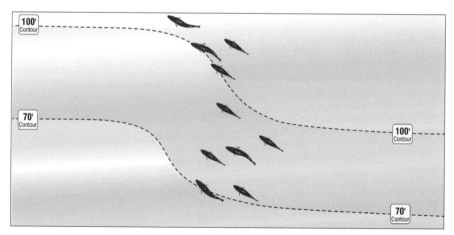

The classic Spot-On-The-Spot rule applies to Great Lakes Chinooks. Subtle nuances in structure, such as a change in the angle of a drop-off, are key areas to locate kings. These angles will deflect bottom currents and attract bait and kings.

Great Lakes anglers pay close attention to their electronics. If you don't watch your electronics closely, you'll miss these features. When you find a spot on your bottom machine, punch in the waypoint and troll through the area a few times. Monitor your graph and mentally map out the microstructure. As you troll over a piece of structure from multiple angles, make notes of the physical dimensions and changes of the structure. While some anglers can mentally remember the texture and shape of these features, a notebook helps! Pay attention to subtle differences in angle, texture and rate of drop on these microstructures. When you locate these treasures, make sure you catalogue the coordinates and make a note of what the weather and sea conditions were like when you caught kings. Chances are good that the location (waypoint) will likely produce fish later that day, later that week and next spring, too.

Deepwater Structure

As mentioned above, the entire water column from east to west and north to south may be hospitable to spring kings. It is easier to locate kings during the spring in less than 140 feet of water. There will be days, however, where kings (open water nomads) will be suspending at random over very deep water. Locating these fish can be difficult. In this scenario, deepwater structure can be a good starting point. These features can be found by consulting topography charts.

Looking for these open water kings is really hunting. When I run offshore spring steelhead trips I will drag one or two lines deep, 50 to 150 feet down. These lines will frequently pop big kings. After a king strike I will slow down and work the area to see if that was a lone king or if a school of kings is present. This strategy is admittedly random but it has resulted in some nice catches of large and unexpected spring kings.

BAITFISH AND SPRING KINGS

Baitfish are always a key ingredient in the chinook equation. While spring kings may not be feeding as frequently as summer fish, they still need to eat. The larger the fish, the more they consume. Pretty profound, eh? Anyhow, schools of alewives will attract spring fish. In May of 2005, on southwestern Lake Michigan, we had giant schools of alewives suspended from 50 to 200 feet down in 180 to 240 feet of water. Guess where we caught lots of kings during May? Way deep, 80 to 150 feet down, in 180 to 240 feet of water. That was open water fishing and the only clues telling you to fish for kings were the giant bait pods lighting

Light line and clean spoons are dynamite for prying spring kings off the bottom.

up the sonar screens. There were also many sea gulls sitting on the water in that area. I have learned over the years that gulls sitting on the water usually indicate that schools of alewives are in the area.

Spring kings will also venture into shallow water (20 to 50 feet) to feed. River outflows, pier heads, harbor mouths and power plant discharges will attract kings. Outflows bring warm water into cold lake water, add nutrients to the food chain and attract baitfish to a region. These features are more appealing to kings if deepwater (over 50 feet) is within one mile of shore. Kings will frequently hold over deep water and make feeding forays into shallower water. The further breakwalls extend into the lake, the more kings they will attract.

Larger rivers will attract more kings into a region than small streams. The best spring king fishing on the Great Lakes occurs each spring on Western Lake Ontario at the mouth of the Niagara River. The Niagara dumps a massive volume of water into Lake Ontario. This river impacts the shoreline region for miles in either direction from the mouth. It also has a huge impact on the offshore waters as it brings large quantities of food into the lake. Huge schools of alewives and feeding kings gather in this region and the fishing is spectacular. Where large rivers are present, look for spring kings to hold along drop-offs in 30 to 50 feet of water offshore from the outflow.

When targeting larger river outflows, look for kings around schools of baitfish. Big kings are eating machines. Areas that have concentrations of alewives will attract kings. For this reason, one eye should be on your graph. If bait is present, you may have the opportunity to target kings. We will take an in depth look at the impact of bait schools on kings in the following chapter.

When searching for spring kings off outflows, target near shore drop-offs and any irregularities in the bottom adjacent to the outflow. Kings will lie close to the bottom along small drops in 20 to 50 feet of water. River runoff is typically warmer than the surrounding lake water so you will want to look for temperature breaks and color lines created by river outflows. Look for kings along the edges of these breaks. Also, when these breaks intersect drop-offs and humps, you will find kings.

In summary, if you are going to catch kings during the spring months, you must target them. You should focus your fishing effort on bottom structure in the 50 to 120 foot range and bait fish. Catching large numbers of spring kings may require you to ignore other species that are more prevalent. While all kings don't relate to bottom features, many, many kings do. By building your spring search patterns around prominent bottom topography, you will greatly increase your chances of locating kings.

CHAPTER 3

Summer Kings: Are You Looking For A Needle In A Haystack?

Let's be honest. Fishing in open water during the heat of the summer can be like looking for a needle in a haystack. The good news, though, is the kings aren't usually scattered equally across all segments of the lake. In fact, the majority of kings off your homeport will usually be concentrated in a few areas. Locating these concentrations of kings will be your key to summer success.

Randomly trolling around, waiting for a bite is not the best way to beat the summer doldrums. Knowing what to look for before you set the first line will lead you to more screaming drags.

Kings move around a lot, but their movements are not random. Kings are guided by significant factors, such as water temperature, bottom structure, baitfish and currents. To zero in on the hot summer action, you need to focus on four factors: cold water, bottom structure, baitfish and currents. If you can find these four elements together, chances are you will find lots of needles, too!

Locating summer kings is often a process of elimination. A four-pronged search criterion will help you eliminate vast tracks of empty water. If you can eliminate unproductive water before you begin fishing, you will spend more time fighting fish and less time hunting!

Using Water Temperature to Eliminate Unproductive Water and Locate Kings

Water temperature is a critical part of the summer king salmon equation. Finding the right temp quickly dials you into a hot bite as you eliminate large areas of unproductive real estate. Before building a water temperature program, let's review some basic biology. King salmon are a cold-blooded creature. While they can survive a range of temperatures, they have a peak operating or efficiency level. God designed them with a built in thermostat that will guide the fish to their preferred temperature range.

Experience has taught us that 42 to 48 degrees is their peak temperature preference. This is the temperature range in which kings thrive. A secondary temp range is 49 to 54 degrees. While big kings like cold water, they will occasionally be found in water as warm as 54 to 58 degrees, especially late in the summer as they prepare to move inshore to spawn.

Do you see the strategy? You have just made the Lake smaller as you have eliminated any water above 54 degrees and colder than 42 degrees!

A healthy understanding of the stratification process of water is the

Captain Dan Keating with the fruit of a successful hunt, a monster summer king.

first step to understanding the world kings live in. This strategy will require you to view the water from a three-dimensional perspective. In your mind you must divide the water column horizontally and vertically.

During the summer months, water in the Great Lakes will stratify. Stratification results in the formation of horizontal layers or bands of water. The warmer layers will be closer to the surface and the colder, denser water will settle deeper in the water column. It should be noted that the thickness of the various bands of differing water temps will not be uniform.

What is the Thermocline?

The thermocline is a major feature of summer stratification. It is one of the dominant features impacting fish movements and is a major form of structure for Great Lakes chinooks. Many charter captains describe the thermocline as the *superhighway* for summer kings. You want to locate the thermocline for two reasons. First, it will help you eliminate unproductive water, as large numbers of kings will not be found above the thermocline. Second, it attracts bait, which attracts kings. Once you locate the depth of the thermocline, everything will be up or down in relation to it. Typically, kings will be located below the thermocline.

What, exactly is the thermocline? During the summer season, the water in the Great Lakes stratifies, much like an inland lake. Layers of warmer water will position themselves toward the surface and as you descend down into the water column, water temps will decrease. A thermocline is the point of transition between warmer water and cold water. Typically, a thermocline features a rapid drop in temperature from about 60 degrees down to 50 degrees. The vertical distance of this drop can vary, in large part, depending on the wind and currents. Some days the vertical distance of the break will cover five feet. In another region, this vertical distance may span 20 feet of the water column.

The thermocline is not static. It is a dynamic break. Over the course of the summer, its location within the water column will vary. For example, if you are 3 miles offshore one particular day, the thermocline may

be 70 feet down; but if you are 5 miles offshore (same day), the thermocline may rise up to 40 feet, or it may drop down to 100 feet. Exact location within the water column will depend on season, local weather,
winds, currents and bottom structure.

The thermocline has a multi-dimensional impact on bait and predator movements. In deep, open water, it is a major piece of structure. Both
kings and baitfish will frequently base their migration patterns in relation to the thermocline.

Since the thermocline attracts large amounts of plankton, it becomes

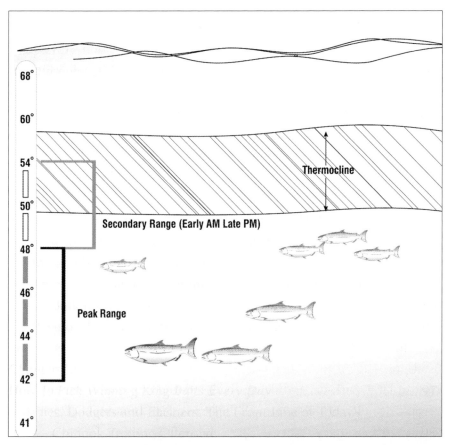

*The thermocline is a key feature helping you locate summer kings. This diagram
illustrates the primary temperature ranges of large kings. Notice, kings will
typically school below the thermocline.*

a major feeding station for alewives. Add some current to the equation and you have a funneling effect that will allow plankton and baitfish to collect.

The thermocline layer also acts as a ceiling. While kings may cross the thermocline to feed, they will typically spend most of their time in the colder layers beneath the thermocline. For this reason, the thermocline is a major piece of structure helping us to eliminate unproductive water.

Using the Thermocline to Zero in On Kings

Once you determine the depth (vertical level) of the thermocline, determine the exact level of the 54-degree water. As you analyze the lake, draw a horizontal line through the water column at that depth. Where this horizontal line intersects the lake bottom, you will then draw a vertical line from the lake bottom up to the surface. The water inside (shallower) this vertical line will be void of kings. In other words, when you leave the harbor and head out, this *intersection* is the shoreward point where you would consider fishing. Likewise, the water above the thermocline will also be too warm to hold kings. You have eliminated any water above the thermocline and inside the point where the thermocline intersects the bottom. Congratulations, you have reduced the size of the lake you are fishing on.

Let's put this strategy into practice. With your three-dimensional glasses in place, your first task is to locate the thermocline. Next, isolate the 54-degree layer. The top edge of 54-degree water is 70 feet down. Next, draw two imaginary lines. The first line runs horizontally through the water column at 70 feet. This line, and the top edge of 54-degree water, intersects the lake bottom in 70 feet of water. The second line is vertical and rises from the lake bottom in 70 feet of water. Where these two lines intersect the bottom, 70 feet of water, is the shoreward point you may want to begin fishing. In other words, you will not find large numbers of kings in less than 70 feet of water or above 70 feet on this day.

This tactic of dividing the water column based on the depth of key water temps will save you hours of valuable time looking for fish because it helps you isolate your target range. Large concentrations of kings will not be found (typically) in water warmer than 54 degrees.

Once you have isolated the thermocline layer, you will want to look down in the water column and locate the 42-degree layer of water. Theoretically, you can find kings anywhere in the 42 to 54-degree layers of water so you need to draw a second horizontal line through the 42-degree layer of water. You now have identified a vertical range (strike box) in which to concentrate your fishing effort by isolating the layers between 42 and 54 degrees.

Now, earlier I said 42 to 48 degrees is the peak temp range for kings. After locating the 42-degree level, locate the upper limit of 48-degree water. The vertical layer of water between 42 and 48 degrees is your primary strike box for large kings. A secondary strike box extends up to the 54-degree band of water. These are the layers you should concentrate your firepower.

I think you understand the picture. During the summer months, water stratifies in horizontal layers. Are all the horizontal layers of water

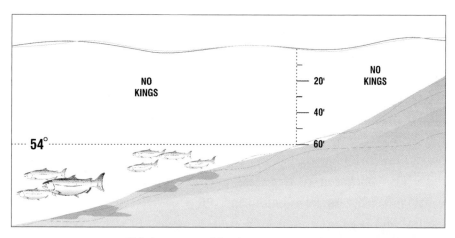

Water temperature will help you quickly eliminate unproductive water. Draw an imaginary line (horizontally) through the water column at the 54-degree level. Where this line intersects bottom, draw a vertical line to the surface. Typically, you will not find kings inside (shoreward) of the vertical line or above the horizontal line.

aligned perfectly even and do they have equal dimensions (thickness)? No. As you move out into the lake, the bands of water will not always be aligned in perfectly horizontal layers. Depending on wind, bottom relief and currents, the bands or layers of water may move down in the water column, or up. Also, the varying temp bands may not exhibit a uniform thickness. For example, the 52-degree layer may be 20 feet thick (vertical) and the 47-degree band may only be 5 feet thick (vertical). For this reason, you will want to monitor or re-check water temps as you change fishing locations in relation to water depth.

How Do You Locate the Thermocline?

You need one tool to help you systematically dissect the water column and locate the thermocline—a sub surface temp probe. If you do not fish

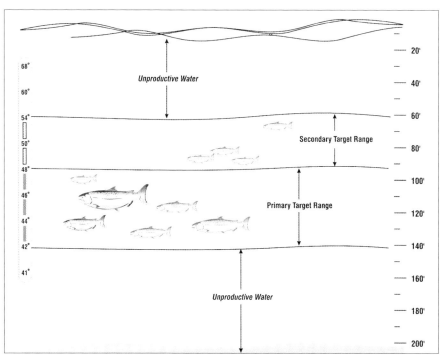

Water stratifies in layers during the summer. When looking for kings, the 42 to 48-degree band of water is the primary target range. A secondary range extends between 48 and 54 degrees.

on a regular basis, this may be the most important piece of equipment on your boat. You can go high tech and use a sub troll or downrigger with a built in temp probe, or you can take the economical route and use a clip-on temp probe, such as Cabelas Temp Finder or the GMT 40. These probes can be attached to your downrigger weight and lowered to depth. After waiting several minutes, the probe can be brought to the surface and the temperature read. The advantage to the electronic probe on your downrigger is that you can continuously monitor the sub surface temperatures as you troll perpendicular to the shoreline and track cold-water bands.

A third technique for locating the thermocline involves using your graph. Many of today's powerful sonars will actually mark the debris field that accompanies the thermocline. This is a quick and easy way to locate the thermocline before putting the first line in the water! When I am under power during the summer, I am constantly observing my graph and watching the level of the thermocline. Many times, I know how far down I need to set my lines before I even slow the boat down.

When the sonar marks the thermocline is the sonar actually detecting a change in water temperature? Or, is the sonar beam bouncing off the cold water? A thermocline is a layer where cold and warm water meet. It is a dividing point. Large amounts of plankton and baitfish will collect along this layer of inversion. Along with the living organisms, dead matter in the water sinks down in the water column and collects along the thermocline. This collection of matter is referred to as a *debris field*. The sound signal transmitted from the transducer is echoing off this layer of dead and living material. The debris field is the fuzzy band you are seeing on your graph.

Generally the debris field, plankton and baitfish will orient themselves horizontally to the thermocline. Many thermoclines will also feature some form of sub-surface current. The turbulence and clutter associated with a strong current will also register on many types of sonar. For a detailed discussion on mounting graphs for optimum performance, see *Great Lakes Salmon And Trout Fishing, The Complete Troller's Guide.*

Exceptions to the Temperature Rule

Before moving on I need to speak out of the other side of my mouth. Cold water (42 to 48 degrees) is my favorite layer for big kings. However, there will be times, especially early and late in the day, when feeding kings will rise up out of the cold water and enter the warmer waters of the thermocline, or slightly above the thermal, to feed. Because of this feeding movement, you may want to run some lines in the 54 to 58-degree band of water at first and last light.

If the water is gin clear, you can also catch many kings that will swim up into the warmer layers to strike a lure. What happens are kings, who often look up and forward, will see a school of bait or your lures above them in warmer water. With a few powerful strokes of their tail, these predators can move up 10 or 15 feet in the water column to nail a quick

The intersection of cold water and baitfish will lead you to kings like this.

meal and quickly retreat back into the cooler depths. I believe many kings are caught each year in warmer water due to increased visibility. Some boats will naturally *raise* kings from the depths. As boats troll through the water, different hulls and props will quite literally attract fish. I believe some kings will be drawn up by this disturbance. These curious fish will venture into warmer water to smash a lure. Now, not all boats have this effect, but many do.

Water temperature also becomes less critical as the spawning urge overtakes adult kings. During August, you will start to encounter increasing numbers of mature kings that may make shoreward movements into warmer water as they begin looking for their stocking and birth sites. These fish will be more aggressive if the water is cold, but warmer water will not stop them from moving shoreward.

BOTTOM STRUCTURE: GUIDEPOSTS TO SUCCESS

Bottom structure is our second major criterion that will point us toward concentrations of summer chinooks. After isolating the vertical layers of the water column holding cold water, you want to locate bottom structure within the cold water range.

Historically, many Great Lakes anglers have ignored the impact of bottom structure on kings. Big mistake! Kings are a structure oriented fish. Whether in 30 feet of water or 200 feet of water, bottom contours will impact fish movements. If it is impacting the fish, it better have an impact on you, too.

Do all king salmon relate their movements to bottom structure? In Chapter 1, I referred to the "Two School Theory" of salmon movements. Without a doubt, school number 1, the nearshore, bottom oriented kings will be more sensitive to bottom structure. Near shore kings, relate much of their movements to structure. Topography, however, will also impact the movements of Offshore Nomads.

Before moving on, let's clear a few myths from the air as I am sure some of you are shaking your heads. King salmon are a Pelagic species.

They are a migratory species that suspend over great depths. Bottom structure frequently determines where these fish will be found suspending. Bottom structure influences currents and baitfish, both of which influence kings. Structure also gives you some great clues to help you locate schools of kings.

What types of bottom variation will attract summer kings? In Chapter 2, I discussed topographical features that attract and hold kings during the spring months. Those same features will hold kings during the summer. However, it is the drop-offs and bank type ledges or hills that are the dominant structural forces during the summer months.

Many of the Great Lakes feature sharp drop-offs that run parallel to the coastlines. These banks or hills funnel water currents and attract big numbers of baitfish and kings during the summer. These very productive drop-offs are typically found in 60 to 200 feet of water.

Why do these large banks attract kings? The attraction is two-fold. First, the drops attract the bait kings feed on. Baitfish, such as alewives, will hold along these drops. Secondly, these banks and drop-offs have a huge impact on the surrounding water. The Great Lakes are full of currents. Bottom currents are magnified and concentrated as they run along the edges of drop-offs. Drop-offs and humps also deflect bottom currents, causing upwellings. These upwellings, in turn, distribute nutrients throughout the water column and attract bait, which attracts predators to all levels of the water column.

Larger drop-offs and humps will have a greater impact on the surrounding region. The currents and upwellings will attract and hold bait and predators to an entire region. Areas up to five miles immediately offshore of these large bank drops are impacted. Frequently large kings will move into the drop-offs early in the morning and hold over deepwater during the mid day. What a beautiful system!

Do all structures attract kings equally? Are small features worth checking out? The answer to these questions depends on the day. While many people assume that larger features attract greater numbers of fish, I learned to appreciate subtle topographical detail while fishing off the coastline of southwestern Florida. The Gulf and Bay waters off the Florida coast appear featureless to the untrained eye.

When I began fishing the shallow Gulf and Bay waters, I ignored the featureless bottom and just assumed there was nothing to concentrate the fish. Was I wrong! After many fish-deficient hours on the water, and much research I learned that incredibly minor variations in the bottom attracted and held bait and Pelagic species in big numbers. Once I learned to focus on these features, my catch rate accelerated greatly.

Upon returning to the Midwest, I applied this mind-set to my home waters on southwestern Lake Michigan. To tell you the truth, I've never fished the same since! I began to pay close attention to my sonar and looked at charts to glean new areas to fish. Many of these previously ignored areas had some minor bottom features. To my great surprise, I discovered many new *Honey Holes* in the 100 to 250 foot range. Because of this valuable lesson I learned in Florida, I expanded my fishing horizon at home, without traveling to a new location.

If the region you fish is essentially void of any major forms of struc-

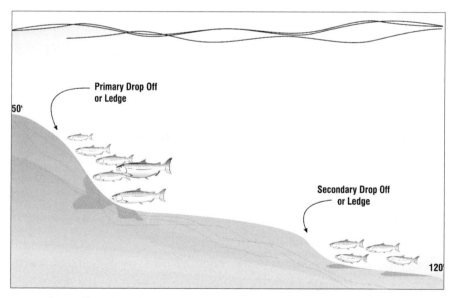

Major drop-offs and bank reefs running parallel to the shoreline in 50 to 200 feet of water are some of the best locations to find summer kings.

ture, then even the mildest changes (3 to 7 feet variation) will attract fish. If you fish off a *structure rich* port, you will have to determine which structures hold fish. In this second scenario you will find that certain structures, while they may appear similar to other local structures, will consistently attract and hold more kings.

When fishing larger structures, look for smaller features or microstructures on or in the vicinity of the dominant feature. These micro-features will frequently hold larger fish and will go unfished by most anglers. Examples of micro features include nipples or indentations in drop-offs, bends in shelfs, the intersection of two ridges or troughs or a change in the angle of a hill or shelf. Rock piles or changes in bottom composition in the vicinity also merit greater attention.

Wrecks sitting on the lake bottom are another terrific king magnet. A variety of sunken vessels can be found scattered across the Great Lakes. Wrecks in 50 to 150 feet are great locations. They deflect bottom currents and attract baitfish. Schools of kings will frequently hang out around wrecks all summer.

Commercial fishing nets are another non-traditional piece of structure.

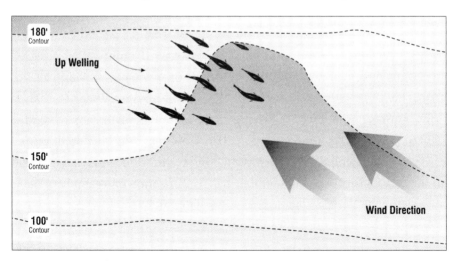

Study the bottom for clues that will lead you to kings. Deep water structures, such as this drop where the 150-foot contour forms a nipple as it comes close to the 180-foot contour, will deflect currents and attract kings to the mid levels of the water column.

Nets function as structure, plus they give off a fish attracting odor and vibrations when struggling fish become entangled. I have made some great catches of kings when trolling parallel to the edges of gill nets. Some of the best action occurs when netters are pulling their nets. Michigan anglers frequently troll around trap nets. These nets will deflect bottom currents. Before trolling around nets, make sure you understand how they are marked and where they are sitting.

Over the course of the summer, the depth you are targeting will change as the cold water and thermocline move up and down in the water column. As the cold water changes location, you will have to target different structures. For example, if the cold water is within two miles of the shore and only 40 feet down, then we will look at bottom contours in the 35 to 120-foot range. If a period of on-shore winds has blown warm water into the region, you may have to run out six miles or more and look down 100 feet to find cold water. When this occurs, you will look for bottom relief in 90 to 250 feet of water.

The longer you spend looking for clues along the bottom, the more *honey holes* you will locate to catch kings. Over time you will build a reference library of productive bottom locations. As you encounter different water temperature profiles and changing weather patterns, you will learn to recognize when individual structures will hold kings. Certain structures will be dynamite on a wind cutting a 45-degree angle off the shore, but when an onshore wind hits, that particular location will be dead. Another local piece of structure will hold fish on an onshore wind but croak when the wind swings off the shoreline. You get the picture— as you isolate hot bottom topography, watch the wind direction and put all the factors together. Different structures will attract kings under varying weather patterns.

THE ROLE OF BAITFISH IN LOCATING KINGS

Big kings are attracted to bait like my six-year-old son, Ethan, is attracted to puddles. When he gets out of the car on a rainy day, he will jump into every puddle between the car and the door. In the same way Ethan is drawn to puddles, big kings will find the bait. Big kings grow big because they stay on the bait. The ramification of this super-size diet is that anglers need to be fishing near bait. If you are fishing in water without bait, the only kings you will encounter will be scattered fish passing through the area.

Bait is highly critical to the survival of large kings during July and August. Mature kings are reaching their peak weights prior to spawning. As these giant fish prepare for the rigorous and physically demanding task of spawning, they are consuming massive amounts of protein. These fish need to eat. Feeding fish are always easier to catch than negative fish. Are you tracking?

The predominant forage across the Great Lakes is alewives. When you think of alewife schools, you should view them as a *form* of structure. Kings will relate their movements and feeding patterns to these bait pods, so treat schools of bait like any other form of structure.

The key to locating schools of bait is a good graph with mid to high-speed resolution. Many of the best tournament anglers and charter captains begin their fishing trips by running and monitoring their graphs for signs of bait. When they mark schools of bait in conjunction with cold water and bottom structure, they will slow down and crisscross the immediate area to gain an idea of just how much bait is present. As they examine the bait pods, they will frequently turn up the gain and look for gamefish marks in and around the bait.

If predators are showing up on the screen, it's a no brainer, set up and begin fishing around the bait pods. If you are not marking game fish, you may elect to set up and troll around the bait pods or continue running. If I slow down on a big school of bait, but fail to mark kings, I will usually run a bit further and look for more bait with game fish marking around the bait.

Schools of alewives frequently will school in bands parallel to the shoreline. If I mark bait pods in 130 feet of water, but no gamefish, I may elect to run parallel to the shoreline in search of more bait. If subsequent schools of bait are void of predator marks, I will then run further off-shore, looking for bait over deeper water. On any given day, you will have to make a decision whether to run to deeper water or look for kings parallel to the shoreline. The right decision will vary from day to day so don't get locked into a formula. Learn to read the water, and *feel* the mood of the fish!

When you mark a school of alewives on your graph, view that school of bait as a form of structure. Make trolling passes in relation to the bait schools from a variety of angles. Let the mood of the fish dictate your trolling passes. If the fish are aggressive (you will often see them slashing across your graph) you will want to troll right over the top of the bait and along the edges. If the fish are sluggish, you will want to work the edges of the schools, making trolling passes that bounce off the bait and work out away from the bait for a ¼ mile. If the kings are dormant, you may want to make trolling passes up to a mile beyond the bait.

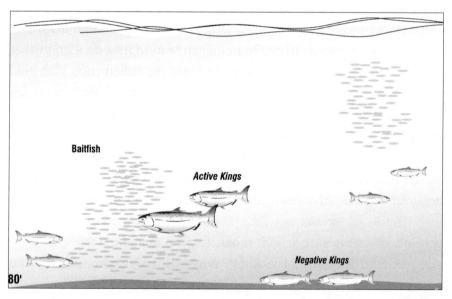

Learn to view schools of alewives as structure. Kings will relate their daily movements and feeding patterns to these bait stacks. After kings feed, they will often shadow the bait and hold close to the bottom.

If you mark kings among the bait but don't get strikes, you may have a presentation problem. Work on your lure selection, lure depths and trolling speeds. Subtle differences in trolling angles can make a huge difference in numbers of strikes. When I run through bait and am marking kings, I like to do neutral drops. I put the boat on top of the fish and drop the engine into neutral for 5 to 15 seconds. Gunning your speed for a few seconds will frequently trigger strikes from reluctant kings. Clean spoons and flies and dodgers will both respond to these speed tactics.

If you don't mark or catch fish, store the bait locations on your GPS and return to the location later in the day. Schools of alewives are like a buffet line to salmon and trout. Just because fish are not present when you are there does not mean kings won't move in on the bait later in the day. Bait schools will often hold in an area and kings will move in on the bait eventually. You don't want to miss the feeding frenzy!

When setting lines around bait pods, target the 42 to 48-degree zone first. If results are slow, don't be afraid to adjust your lure depths and try working various layers around the bait. When big schools of bait are holding in warm water that is close to cold water, kings will move out of temperature to feed. Also, don't ignore the layers beneath the bait, as larger kings will often hang below and outside bait pods.

A common scenario on nice, calm summer days is for kings to shadow schools of alewives. When this occurs, you will mark large pillars of bait but, you will not see a king on your sonar. Kings will frequently sit just outside these bait schools (1/4 to 1 mile) and hold tight to the bottom. You will never mark these negative kings, but they are there. Kings that are shadowing bait pods often need to be finessed off the bottom. This can be done with clean spoons on light line run on downriggers, wire line Dipsies with flies and dodgers or with wires and ball weights.

Alewife schools come in many sizes. Depending on the year, season and local weather patterns you may encounter small, isolated bait pods or you may run into large blocks of water that appear filled with bait pods. Either scenario will attract kings. If you are trolling far offshore over deep water, a lone school of bait in the middle of nowhere will draw kings. Offshore Nomads will swarm these isolated schools of bait. Tight trolling passes should be made to capitalize on this situation.

Baitfish are a key ingredient to locating summer kings. They may be the most important variable leading to success. Don't panic if you find big schools of bait but don't catch fish. At times, patience is required and you just need to wait for feeding kings to hit the bait. If you begin fishing during the afternoon (my favorite time to catch summer kings) and mark schools of bait in 70 to 140 feet of water, you may want to run offshore and fish for suspended fish. As the sun begins to settle and light penetration decreases, it is time to move back into the bait schools and wait for the late afternoon and evening king bite. It can be a very exciting time of day on the water.

CURRENTS: THE MYSTERIOUS VARIABLE INFLUENCING SUCCESS

The average Big Water angler gives very little thought to currents when looking for kings. In my last book, *Great Lakes Salmon And Trout Fishing, The Complete Troller's Guide,* I said that currents are one of the least understood variables in Great Lakes salmon and trout fishing. I'm going to say it again here, because it bears repeating—most anglers minimize the impact of currents on fish migration patterns, daily movements and lure selection.

While you can't see currents with your eye, you can measure their impact on fish, the water and trolling lines. Currents are a major variable dictating the locations and migration patterns of bait and predators. If you understand how wind and currents move water in the Great Lakes, you can use these variables to help you locate kings. You will also learn that currents have a huge impact on lure presentation and the group dynamic.

The majority of currents in the Lakes are the product of wind and weather. Because they are wind driven, their velocity, direction and duration will change over time. A second type of current is the result of the Earth's rotation. This is referred to as the Coriolis Effect and will be examined below.

Attributes of Great Lakes Water

Step into the classroom for a minute. The Great Lakes are unlike any other body of water in the world. While the Lakes are tremendously large they lack many of the oceanic attributes of the Seas. They are not governed by tides, lack salinity and they do not have large, one-directional oceanic currents like the Gulf Stream. Similar to the oceans, the Lakes contain massive amounts of deep, open water. The Great Lakes contain roughly 20 percent of the world's fresh surface water! They are characterized by a variety of surface and sub surface currents and they experience

Giant summer kings are the result of hard work.

upwellings. The upwellings can lead to massive transfers or inversions of water masses.

Despite their great size, the Lakes also exhibit some of the characteristics of smaller inland lakes. A thermocline sets up during the summer months and the Lakes go through a fall turnover period similar to what is seen in smaller bodies of water. The net result is that the water and currents of the Great Lakes are unique. Observant anglers have learned to decipher the impact of currents on bait and predator locations. You can learn, too.

Currents and Their Impact on The Great Lakes

Water in the Great Lakes is not static. Because of the Lakes unique attributes and the diverse weather patterns of the region, water within the individual Lakes actually *moves around* significantly more than inland lakes.

The dominant currents found in the Great Lakes are wind driven. They are the product of extended periods of wind. The implication of this is that currents can change direction and velocity. For example, a Southwest wind will blow at 15 knots for several days. This wind will generate a current along the surface of the Lake and the surface water will flow or move from South/Southwest to the North/Northeast. This is called a *surface push*. The stronger the wind the greater the push. Often, the push will increase in the afternoon as winds strengthen. The surface push primarily impacts water in the upper third of the water column.

Because the Great Lakes are "not that big," this surface current will ultimately hit the opposite shoreline. This forces the water along the leeward shoreline down in the water column. As water continues to pile into the shoreline, the "original" shoreline water is displaced and flows in the opposite direction along the bottom. This results in a *reverse current*. The reverse current typically runs 180 degrees opposite the surface current. The reverse current will impact the bottom third to one half of the water column. Velocity variations between surface and reverse currents can be quite drastic.

The intersection between reverse currents and major drop-offs are key areas to locate feeding kings. Drop-offs will deflect bottom currents and can actually cause a reverse current to move at a variety of angles to the surface current. Large, bank type drop-offs will also magnify reverse currents. For example, say there is a strong reverse current flowing from north to south along the bottom third of the lake. When this current comes into contact with a sharp drop-off in 60 to 120 feet of water, this current will be much stronger along the drop-off. As you move away from the drop-off, the current will diminish.

Many anglers notice they are in a region of strong currents when their downrigger cables start criss-crossing or hanging off to the side of the boat. Many of the speed-at-depth probes will help you to determine the angles and velocities of sub surface currents and reduce guess work.

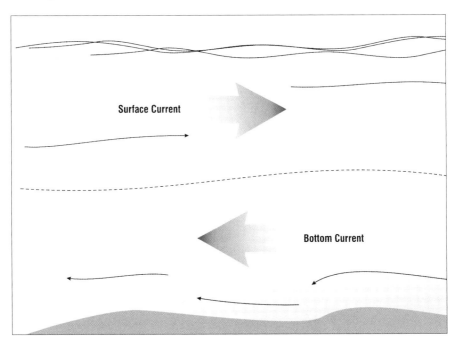

Water in the Great Lakes is not static. Currents play a major role in predator and bait locations. This diagram illustrates what many anglers know as a reverse current. In this diagram, the current running along the bottom is moving in the opposite direction to the surface current.

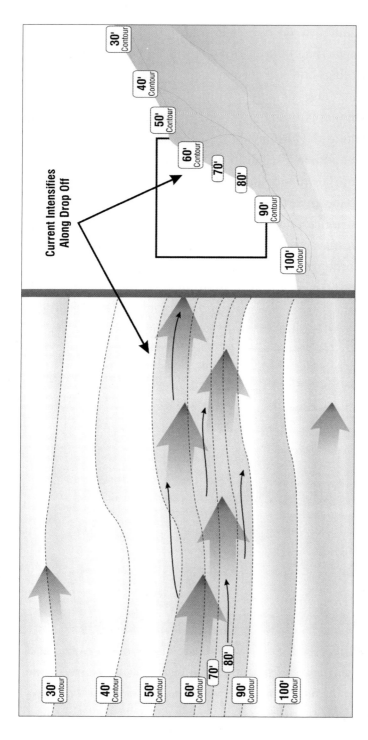

When currents come into contact with sharp drop-offs, the current intensifies along the drop. These currents funnel bait and attract kings. When fishing areas with strong currents, anglers must fine-tune their trolling speeds and angles to catch kings.

You can also measure a current by using a GPS to track your trolling direction. A GPS measures your movement over the bottom, not through the water. For example, let's say you are trolling through the water on a westerly course (270 degrees). Your compass says you are pointed 270 degrees, but your GPS says you are moving over the bottom at a 300-degree heading. What's happening? Your compass and your GPS suggests you're moving in two different directions? A northbound surface current is impacting your trolling path. While your boat may be pointed west (270 degrees) the surface current is pushing you in a northerly direction. If you learn to track your trolling direction over the bottom, you will quickly understand the impact of currents. In this scenario you will have to increase trolling speed and point the boat on a southwest compass heading to move at a 270-degree line (angle) over the bottom. Cutting the current is critical to success.

A second type of current influences water in the Lakes as well. This second current is the result of the Coriolis Effect. Little research has been done on the impact of the Coriolis on the Great Lakes. The Coriolis Effect is a current resulting from the Earth's rotation. Because of the Earth's spin, large bodies of water in the northern hemisphere feature a clock-wise rotation of water. The Coriolis current is felt primarily on the surface water. Because of the Lakes unique size, a reverse current can set up beneath the Coriolis current. The Coriolis current is subtle, and a strong wind blowing against the Coriolis current, will diminish and overpower the Coriolis current. It is easier to measure the impact of the Coriolis within three miles of the shoreline. The Coriolis Effect seems to magnify northbound surface currents.

Upwellings

The Great Lakes also feature upwellings. Upwellings are the result of current deflection. Basically, an upwelling occurs when a strong current running along the bottom hits a drop-off, shelf or shoreline. When the current hits the obstruction, it is deflected upwards, toward the surface. Upwellings take nutrients from cold water layers and bring them up into the upper layers of the water column. Upwellings are also responsible for taking cold water from the bottom and redistributing it into shoreline regions and the upper layers of the water column. Great Lakes anglers refer to this transfer of cold water as *rolling*.

Thermoclines, Currents and Basic Water Movement

As I said above, the thermocline is a key feature you want to locate when looking for summer kings. Let's unpack the dynamics of the Great Lakes thermocline. For starters, it is not static, but will actually change its vertical location, with respect to the water column, depending on the wind direction and velocity. In other words, it will move up and down in the water column from one day or week to the next. The depth (within the water column) of the thermocline may also vary from one location to the next as you move perpendicular to the shoreline. For example, if offshore winds dominate, you may find the thermocline down 30 feet in 60 feet of water but out in 200 feet it may be down 90 feet. With onshore winds you may find the thermocline down 90 feet in 110 feet of water but only 50 feet down in 200 feet.

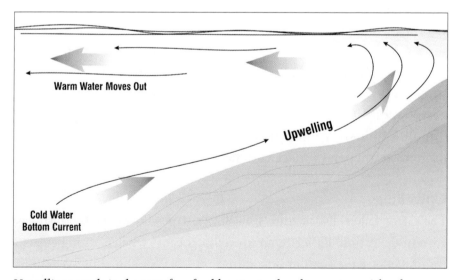

Upwellings result in the transfer of cold water to shoreline regions. A local upwelling will influence the location of kings.

Wind driven currents are the main force impacting thermocline location. Extended periods of onshore winds will push warm surface water
into a region. The surface push or current will "pile" this warm water up
along the downwind shoreline. As the warm water hits the coast, it will

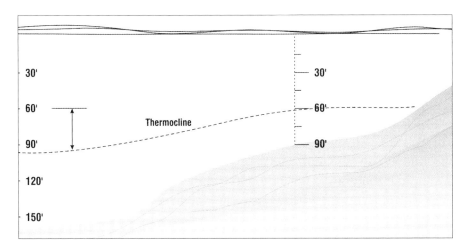

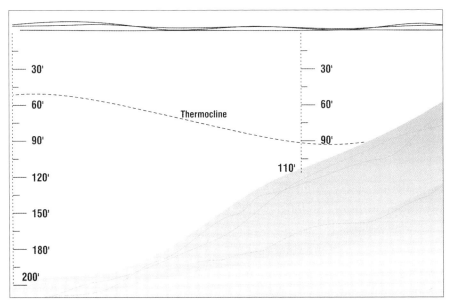

The location of the thermocline will often change its location (vertically) as you
move perpendicular to the shore. Winds and currents dictate the location and
movement of the thermocline.

displace the colder water and force the cold water down and out along the Lake bottom. When this scenario sets up, the thermocline will be driven deeper into the water column. If the onshore winds last for an extended period and if large amounts of super warm surface water have accumulated, the thermocline may also move further offshore.

Because the wind and currents steer the location of the thermocline, it is very easy to predict and anticipate the location of summer kings. If an extended period of onshore winds hit your homeport during the summer, you will know, before you leave the harbor, that the cold water will be driven offshore and down in the water column. You can assume that you will need to fish over deep water if you want to catch kings. How far down in the water column cold water is driven will depend on the velocity and duration of the onshore winds. Fifteen to twenty-five miles per hour onshore winds for three days will move a lot of water. Twenty-four hours of the same wind will have a lesser impact.

If an offshore wind prevails, the opposite will occur. When extended periods of offshore winds take hold of a region a strong surface current will take hold. This surface current will push the warm surface waters out into the lake. This will result in an upwelling of deeper, colder water. The cold water, which is located offshore along the bottom, will creep along the bottom layers of the water column and move toward the shoreline. As the cold water hits near shore drop-offs, shallows and the shoreline, it moves up and takes the place of the warm water that has blown out into the lake.

Offshore winds will push the thermocline higher up in the water column as you move shoreward. In many regions, the thermocline may move very close to the shoreline. With extended periods of offshore winds, you will usually get a very inconsistent thermocline. You may find icy cold 44 to 50-degree water right next to the shoreline on an August afternoon. As you move offshore, the thermocline will actually descend down into the water column. As you approach offshore structure, you will find "spikes" where the thermocline and cold water will rise up in the water column, and then drop back down. Small boat anglers love this sce-

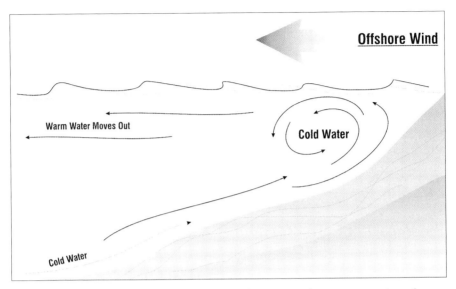

An extended period of offshore wind will push warm surface water out into the lake. Cold water will move in along the bottom to replace the warm water. This is referred to as rolling.

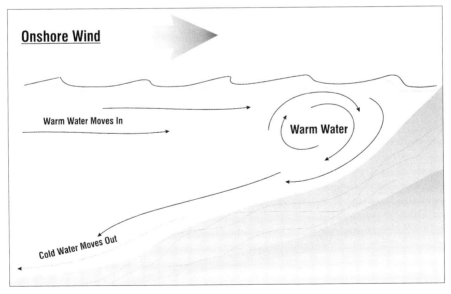

An onshore wind has the opposite affect. It will drive warm surface water into a region. Cold water will move down and out, forcing the thermocline down into the water column.

nario because schools of alewives and kings will frequently follow the cold water into shoreline regions.

Many people believe that an offshore wind blowing at a 90-degree angle to the shore will have the strongest impact on currents and water movement. Actually, when the wind blows offshore at about a 45-degree angle (with respect to the shoreline), you will get maximum currents and water movement. In some locations, a wind of 20 knots or greater, running parallel to the shoreline will bring the greatest upwelling of cold water inshore.

The Impact of Currents on King Movements

Savvy king anglers will use the currents to help determine the location of cold water and baitfish. Water in the Great Lakes will often move in mass. Because of the Lakes unique properties, warm and cold water masses or layers can actually change location quite rapidly. The currents can actually move a mass of warm water into a region and displace a

Currents are one of the least understood variables on the Great Lakes. Understanding currents will help you to locate kings.

mass of cold water, and vice versa. This has a huge impact on fishing for two main reasons. First, alewives are weak swimmers. When a strong current sets up and moves water around, alewives will move with the current. Secondly, kings are very temperature sensitive. They will change location in the lake depending on water temperatures. If the water is too warm, kings will vacate a region.

Remember, if you want to catch big kings during the summer, you must find cold water and bait fish. Currents are the dominant force responsible for the location of cold water. Monitoring the wind direction and velocities in the days leading up to a fishing trip will help you locate kings. Learn to read the currents and monitor how various winds and currents impact your local fishery. A deeper understanding of these features will give you an intuitive approach when searching for kings. You can learn to anticipate the movements of kings before you even set a line!

CHAPTER 4

The Hunt For Autumn Kings

Autumn is a magical season across the Great Lakes. It is a time when an explosion of color ripples across the countryside, the pulse rate of hunters quickens as they prepare for the hunt . . . and the mighty king salmon continue their march with destiny as they enter shoreline regions to spawn. Historically, some of the best king fishing takes places during the fall. Two distinct fisheries are available during September and October.

First, you have the near shore fishery for mature, spawning bound kings. This near shore fishery gives many small boat anglers an excellent opportunity to intercept migrating schools of mature chinooks.

Secondly, you have the offshore fishery for immature kings that some hardy anglers pursue through November into December. This fishery is relatively new and many Great Lakes anglers are not aware it exists. In some regions, the best fishing will be miles from shore, but in other locations, schools of 3 to 15 pound kings can be found a mile off the shore during the late fall.

PRE-SPAWN KINGS IN SHALLOW WATER

My first taste of shallow water chinook fishing was when I was in grade school. After a summer of chasing coho, steelhead and lakers, my dad and I decided we were ready to move up to the big leagues. Early one

September morning, dad hooked up our 17-foot Boston Whaler, the *Frick N' Frack,* to the back of the white station wagon and we headed down to Burnham Harbor on Chicago's lake front. You have to understand, when I was growing up, the mayor of Chicago loved fishing and he made sure Chicago's harbors were stocked with loads of kings.

I truly don't think we were prepared. After hours of trolling between rolling and jumping Leviathans it finally happened—I started screaming and my dad jumped out of my way. Finally, one of those bronze monsters we'd been waiting for hit one of our lines. The fight was on! It was quickly obvious that our small spinning reel and soft rod was outgunned, but we had a blast! My dad and I were hooked on autumn chinook fishing.

Ever since that first strike—autumn took on a whole new meaning to a young boy growing up in the western suburbs of Chicago. No longer was fall marked by the approaching gloom of school and the loss of days of summer spent exploring, swimming, fishing, building forts or riding bikes. Now, cool nights and the start of school meant my dad and I were

going to catch huge fish! Monday through Friday found me daydreaming about the upcoming Saturday morning king trips. The cruelest thing my father ever did was to take work colleagues fishing during the week and leave me in school. In my imagination, I was right there on the boat with my dad and his friends. In reality, however, I was spacing out in the classroom, daydreaming about trophy chinooks and smoking drags. I would race home from school to see the monsters he

Dan cut his teeth early on kings.   would drag home from the lake!

The months of September and October are great times for small boat anglers and novices with limited big water experience to catch trophy kings. Compared to spring and summer fishing, the tactics to locate and catch spawning bound kings are relatively simple. Another plus is you don't need a lot of extra equipment. In fact, with a relatively small selection of lures, anyone can catch numbers of kings during the fall.

Let me illustrate the simplicity of fall king fishing from the perspective of a couple of 16 year olds. When my *partner in crime,* Paul Jaros and I turned 16, and procured our drivers licenses, we developed our own unique system for catching kings. Our vessel was Paul's old canoe and our tackle selection was limited to two rods, based on carrying capacity. Unlike today, we were never confused on lure selection as we usually only had a handful of lures in the canoe. Despite these apparent limitations, we made some awfully impressive catches from that canoe. But our techniques were not rocket science. My point being, if you are new to king salmon fishing, fall is a great time to gain experience, catch a few big fish and build confidence you can carry to open water next summer.

Do Your Homework Before You Go Fishing

Locating spawning bound kings in shallow water is not difficult. Much of the *fish finding* occurs before you leave the dock. First, you must understand that spawning bound kings are not distributed equally across the Great Lakes. King salmon are an amazing creature and they return to their exact spawning or stocking location. In their indigenous Pacific coast environment kings migrate across thousands of miles of open-ocean and reach the precise river system of their birth. These fish will then migrate hundreds of miles inland to the very tributary of their birth. In the Yukon River, kings will actually swim over a thousand miles inland to spawn!

If you want to catch chinooks in shallow water during the fall, you need to target river and harbor mouths where they were planted or hatched naturally. Yes, some kings do stray, so theoretically you can encounter a trophy king any where along the shoreline, but you will burn more drags if you fish off stocking and native reproduction sites. Since spawning bound kings are preoccupied with reproduction, water temperature and baitfish, two primary search criterion during the summer months are no longer the primary factors guiding your quest for kings.

Consequently, being in the right location is critical to success with spawning bound kings. Remember, when the biological clock ticks, it's time for kings to head home. Your first step to locating kings is to consult DNR stocking figures. The majority of Great Lakes kings mature in their third and fourth year so you want to target locations that received heavy plantings during the prior two to four years. Today, some rivers and streams on Lakes Michigan, Superior, Huron and Ontario feature runs of kings that are reproducing naturally. Plan your autumn fishing adventures off harbors and rivers that have good numbers of returning kings.

KNOW YOUR OPPONENT:
HOW DOES MR. CHINOOK BEHAVE?

OK, you've determined where you need to launch your boat, now what? How do you find spawning bound kings in shallow water? Are the same criteria you used to locate kings during the spring and summer applicable or do new rules govern the hunt? Is deep water still an option, or should you concentrate your efforts on the shoreline? As you develop a philosophy of locating kings, you must always remember the attributes of your target. *The identity and characteristics of your target should determine your philosophy of locating kings.*

King salmon, like all salmon, are unique because they have three very different stages in their life. Life begins in a river where young kings spend roughly the first six months of life. Stage two leads them to a large body of water (the Great Lakes) where they mature and the final stage of life leads them back into shallow water and their river of origin. Their environment, physiology and behavior are very different during all three stages.

Spawning kings are not the same fish you encountered in open water. A large king in clear, deep, open water will behave very differently than a king in 20 feet of water. The purpose and orientation of life for spawning bound kings are unlike summer kings that were focused exclusively on feeding and seeking out cold water. Spawning bound kings are on a mission. Their sole focus becomes reproduction. Feeding is no longer the driving force in their life.

Physiologically, kings go through some substantial changes in order to spawn. From an angler's perspective, the most notable change is their apparent loss of appetite. As kings advance in the spawning process, their stomachs atrophy and they quit feeding. What does this tell an angler? Feeding is no longer a trigger mechanism. The implication being, baitfish and cold water are no longer key factors in locating kings. Most of the fall kings you encounter off river and harbor mouths will not be feeding. Kings fresh in from deep water may have a minimal interest in feeding, but as the spawning urge advances, feeding becomes a distant memory.

Other physiological changes impacting king behavior occur in their bodies. As kings mature, they expend a great deal of energy growing the egg sacs and milt that will continue the survival of their species. Their

Staging kings behave differently than summer kings! Different tactics are needed.

bodies develop a protective mucus layer and their once silvery sides fade to shades of golden-brown, olive, red and black. The development of canine teeth and hooked jaws give these fish a menacing appearance.

Kings, like other salmon, are very social and aggressive during the mating season. For this reason, they will be highly concentrated. The majority of fish returning to a particular river or harbor will hold in key areas before moving upriver to spawn. Find these locations or *sweet spots*, and it is time to have some fun.

Location, Location, Location

Remember my story of catching kings from a canoe with minimal tackle selection? The real key to those early successes was the fact that Paul and I stumbled across key fish holding locations. The major concentrations of big, spawning bound kings will always be found staging off a few select locations. Every river and harbor mouth has a few sweet spots. Once you find where the kings hold, catching them is not difficult, really!

The three primary factors to key your search on are current flow, physical structure (natural and man-made) and close proximity to the spawning river, stream or harbor. When kings first show up off river and harbor mouths, they bunch up. Yes, kings come back in waves and when waves first hit the shoreline, fish will be spread out. But as the run advances, the fish become highly concentrated.

Since kings use their acute sense of smell to guide them home, current or water flow attracts and holds fish. Rivers with strong flow rates tend to host strong runs of fish. After large rains, flow rates increase and waves of kings are frequently drawn home like bears to honey. For this reason, the days following large low-pressure systems with heavy rain will produce great action off river mouths.

When river runoff hits the lake, it takes on a life of its own as shoreline currents and wind driven currents will typically push the water in one direction, either parallel to the shore or out into the lake. This water is often murky or stained and is easy to locate with the naked eye. The water temp within the discharge is usually warmer than the surrounding lake water. Look for kings in the areas being washed by the current flow (river discharge).

Since river plumes are guided by local winds and currents you may find fish north of a particular river one weekend and return the following week to find the fish off the south side of the river (or east and west depending on the orientation of the shoreline). Color lines created by outflows are also great structures to troll along. Typically, the fish are following the flow.

The second step to locating kings is to find the natural and man-made structures that come into direct contact with the current flow. The edges of deep holes immediately off river mouths are usually the number one spot to find kings. Other key structures to focus on include break walls, piers and jetties, drop offs, wave troughs, depressions, rip rap and humps. Look for those features that are in direct contact with the river or stream flow and you will find kings.

When kings enter shoreline regions they will hold near structure.

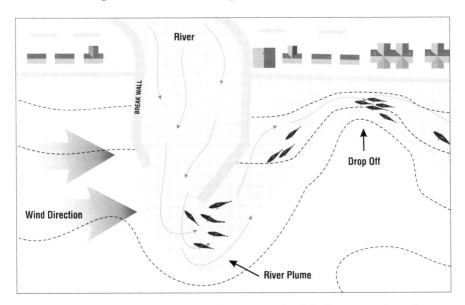

When looking for pre-spawn kings off river mouths, fish the areas where the river plume washes over structure such as pier heads, drop offs, wave troughs and deep holes.

Kings that are staging to run up a river will often hold along drop-offs in 8 to 40 feet of water. The closer a drop is to the harbor or river, the better. Early in the run (August and early September) when kings are still looking for their spawning river or harbor, they will key their movements off near shore drop-offs within several miles of the river mouth. If you have not fished off a port, you may want to consult a topo chart and isolate some structure features.

Catching large numbers of mature kings boils down to your ability to identify the key areas holding fish. It's not rocket science. If the fish are holding in one, two or three small locations, you are dealing with a small strike zone. The more time you spend hitting the strike zone, the more fish you will catch. Repeat after me, "maximum contact with the strike zone yields maximum numbers of strikes." For this reason, small boat anglers have a huge advantage over larger boats that require more space to turn. Maneuverability is a great tool in the fall as short, tight passes are often the best tactic. Chapter 14 looks at specific techniques for catching kings in the shallows.

Fall fishing can be stressful. Often you will be dealing with large numbers of boats all trying to fish in the same spot. Common sense is frequently checked at the dock, so be patient and courteous. Remember, you are not the only person fishing. When trolling, monitor the locations and trolling directions of other boats. Gauge your distance from others with respect for turning radius and trolling patterns. It only takes one bad egg going against the flow to spoil a good thing. Weekdays are usually less crowded as are mid-day and late afternoon hours. Shallow water kings can be caught throughout the day. I have experienced many charters where the afternoon trips out-produced the morning trips when fishing river mouths.

OFFSHORE OPTIONS FOR IMMATURE KINGS

The fall months also give anglers a chance to target immature kings that are not spawning. These fish will typically weigh from 2 to 15 lbs. In some regions 20 lb. kings will be caught as well. This fishery spans the months of September and October, but some anglers fish kings through November into December. The fishery is weather related and strong winds can keep you off the lake at any time during the fall.

This discussion about locating immature kings during the fall will be limited as the tactics and philosophy are similar to the summer and spring months. In some regions summer patterns will govern the hunt well into September. If a thermocline is still in place, then you will continue to hunt for schools of kings like you would during July and August. In this scenario, winds will be a key factor determining *where* you will look for fish. Remember, extended periods of onshore winds will drive cold water and kings deep. Offshore winds will bring cold water closer to the surface and the shoreline. Just like summer fishing, you will look for the intersection of cold water (42 to 48 degrees), baitfish, bottom structure and current.

Another variable that will draw immature kings shoreward during September and early October is the migration of adult fish. When adult kings begin staging offshore of spawning sites over deep water, juvenile kings will follow the big guys. As the spawners move shoreward, some immature kings will follow them. Some of these fish will go all the way into the beach, but many of these fish will find cold water and bait in 30 to 60 feet of water. If cold water and bait holds, these immature fish will stay in the shallows all of September and October. If the water warms or bait is scarce, the immature kings will retreat to the depths as adult fish hit the pier heads. This pattern will vary from year to year, but some years, it will result in very good fishing.

As fall advances and onshore winds increase, kings have a tendency to go deep late in the year. Some seasons winds will pile massive amounts of warm water into a region. When this occurs you may be chasing kings 100 to 150 feet down. During the fall I have caught kings over 200 feet deep! Under these conditions, look for the intersection of 48-degree water and the bottom. This is where you should begin looking for kings.

Another late season scenario that can wreak havoc on the Great Lakes is wild and constantly shifting wind regimes. Under this pattern cold and warm fronts will bombard an area resulting in shifting winds that will oscillate back and forth. This tends to mix up the water and experience shows kings will retreat offshore to deepwater realms eight miles or more from shore. Currents tend to be more intense close to shore and offshore realms will be more stable under shifting wind patterns.

Under this pattern, you will be hunting for open water kings over deep water. Look for cold water and baitfish. Large schools of small, young of the year alewives will often be found over deepwater during autumn. These schools are easy to locate with sonar and will attract immature kings. You may want to consult Chapter 9, as the principles discussed will work during the late autumn.

Immature kings can extend your fishing season well into the fall!

The wild card during the fall is weather. The Great Lakes region tends to have unstable weather during the fall and rapidly changing weather will move fish around. While warm and cold water still exist early in the fall, the thermocline continues to be a major barrier of demarcation leading you to kings. Once the thermocline dissipates, you will be facing Lakes that look very similar to the springtime. Late in the autumn, you will want to hunt for kings as if it were spring.

Lure Selection and Integration for Great Lakes Kings

The Art of Lure Selection

"Give a man a Filet O' Fish sandwich and he won't be hungry for a day. Teach him how to fish and he'll feed himself for life."

—THE UNKNOWN ANGLER

If you understand the how and why involved in choosing lures and setting lines, you will make wise decisions on the water and you will catch more trophy kings. What is the alternative? You can read last week's fishing tips and be a day late!

CHAPTER 5

A Philosophy Of Lure Selection

Is lure selection and integration something you can learn? Or is it a product of gut instinct? After all, some anglers just seem to pick the right lures day after day after day. What stands behind the decisions these guys make? Is it luck? Science? Instinct? Experience?

Before you look at what other anglers do, I want to ask you a question. With the tremendous variety of lures, attractors and color combinations available, what leads you to select one lure over another? How do you determine which delivery applications to use?

Are your decisions based on instinct? Past experience? A local fishing report? Weather conditions? Or, is lure selection for you an impulsive, random exercise, similar to playing *pin the tail on the donkey*? Like a child at a party, you place a blindfold across your eyes (ignoring all available data), spin around (ignoring the conditions of the day), and arbitrarily choose a lure and drop it somewhere in the water?

Learning how to select and run lures is hugely important to success. But picking lures is much more involved than reading another person's list of hot baits. You know the old saying, "Give a man a *Filet O' Fish* sandwich and he won't be hungry for a day, teach a man *how* to fish and he'll feed himself for life." Lure selection is a learning process that lasts a lifetime.

If you understand the *how* and *why* involved in choosing baits and setting lines you will make wise decisions on the water. You will learn to react to your environment, weather, time of day and the moods of the fish. Experience and practice will lead you to a deeper understanding of the lure selection process. In time, it will become second nature and eventually require little thought. Yes, instinct often trumps common sense and reason on the water, but the *art* of lure selection becomes part of your unique fishing style and strategy. What is the alternative? You can read last week's fishing tips in the local paper and be a day late, or you can learn the mechanics of lure selection.

FIVE FUNDAMENTAL PRINCIPLES TO GUIDE LURE SELECTION FOR ONCORHYUCHUS TSHAWYTSCHA

Walk into any tackle store or peruse a catalog and it is easy to become overwhelmed by the tremendous variety of lures available. If you take a

systematic approach to lure selection and understand the mechanics involved in running a variety of lures, you can learn how to choose winning lure combos. As this is a twofold process you need to understand the attributes that differentiate individual lures and the variables impacting a lures performance. Understanding the mood of the fish helps, too.

When selecting a lure for kings, consider the characteristics that make it appealing. Individual lures and brands have unique properties that

If you learn how to choose lures, you will catch kings under all conditions.

set them apart from other baits. Some baits will be dynamite on coho but may rarely catch a king. What are the characteristics that set stud king baits apart from the pack?

You also need to understand what variables determine whether a big king will smash a magnum green dolphin Silver Streak one moment and then take a chewed-up aqua fly and silver dodger and ignore that hot spoon the next day. If you want to make wise lure selections, then focus on five principles that impact every lure related decision.

Principle 1: The Role of Target Depth and Lure Visibility

Different lure types (spoons, flies, plugs) and individual brands of lures appeal to kings at different levels of the water column. When you change baits, you need to select lures from the fish's perspective—not the perspective of an impulsive shopper or a captain who hasn't had a strike in an hour. The appearance and effectiveness of individual lures varies depending on the target depth they are trolled. Light penetration varies by depth, water clarity, sky and sea conditions. Basically, the deeper into the water column you descend, the darker the environment becomes. Therefore, a silver spoon with a green edge looks different 40 feet down than it does 90 feet down.

What does this mean? Baitfish and your lures and attractors look different at various levels within the water column. In reality, some lures and attractors will look more authentic or appealing at different levels within the water column. For example, a purple Michigan Stinger may look like the real deal to a king 82 feet down, but at the 30-foot level, it looks like a thin piece of metal painted purple. The same king suspended 30 feet down may reject the purple Stinger, but be all over a Caramel Dolphin Dreamweaver. Why? Because the different color and different action of the Dreamweaver are mimicking the natural forage of the bait Mr. Chinook is chasing at a specific depth.

Target depth also impacts whether or not you should run an attractor. For example, you may need to run flashers and flies to trigger bites for kings 80 to 120 feet down, but kings holding 50 to 70 feet down might only strike clean spoons on the same day. *The depth you are targeting is critical to lure selection and should have a huge impact on the types and colors of lures and attractors you select.*

Principle 2: The Trigger Mechanism of Chinooks Changes with Location

Where you are fishing impacts lure selection. Chinooks behave differently from one location in the water column to another. For example, a king salmon suspended 92 feet down over 240 feet of water is a very different fish than a king hugging bottom in 70 feet or a king running the shoreline in 12 feet of water. The immediate environment of the fish has a huge impact on their behavior. If kings are in ultra clear water, they will react differently than if they are in shallow, murky water. If their behavior and environment are varied, then you will have to rely on a selection of lures to catch fish in different regions and layers of the lake.

Let's just think about this for a minute. When you are headed home after a hard day on the water, do you always feel like stopping at McDonalds for the same old hamburger and fries? Do you ever feel like Taco Bell one day or Subway the next? Just like different foods appeal to you and me from day to day, different baits appeal to kings from one day to the next. From a king's perspective one lure is more appealing in 35 feet of water and a very different lure is more appealing 100 feet down in 180 feet of water. Lure selection must appeal to the trigger mechanism of the fish based on the immediate environment of the fish.

Principle 3: Target Depth Impacts Color Selection

Lure color is determined by how far down in the water column you are fishing. I referenced this point during a seminar I gave in Michigan and two of the most accomplished Captains on the Great Lakes came up to me and said, "We do exactly what you do, but we never hear anyone else talk about it." Seasoned veterans internally know that target depth impacts lure color. Rarely will they discuss it openly!

Light penetration is different at each level in the water column. Some colors will be highly visible at 30 feet, but not at 80 feet. So, if you find kings suspending over a broad depth spectrum, let's say from 30 feet down to 100 feet, the best color bait to run at 30 feet will be different than the color to run at 75 feet. In practice, if a 75-foot rigger is on fire and you want to get a Dipsy at 35 feet to produce, chances are, you won't put the exact same color on the shallow rod. You may use the same brand and size lure, but a different color will produce more of the shallower kings.

When selecting lures ask yourself how deep they will be running. Target depth should determine color selection. *Folks, this concept is radical, but it will lead you to more kings.*

Principle 4: The Team Concept

Lure location within the group dynamic impacts performance. First, not all individual lures work equally well on all delivery devices. Secondly, some individual lures work better when they are run in conjunction with other lures. The practical application of this is that when assigning lures to various locations within the group dynamic, you need to recognize which individual lures produce kings off a Dipsy Diver but not on a downrigger. Different lures will work on downriggers but not on wire divers. As you identify which lures work *where* within your group dynamic, you will learn which group of lures to use on downriggers, which group to use on Dipsies, leadcore, etc.

A second element to the group dynamic is what makes some lures so productive when run in combination with other individual lures. This is the team philosophy inherent within the group dynamic. The Green Bay Packers had a fantastic combination of players in Bret Favre and Sterling Sharpe. This combination knew how to move the ball down the field and score. When you are fishing, you will develop combinations of lures and delivery devices that will produce fantastic results over and over again. You are the coach and you need to identify these *teams* and learn under what conditions to use them.

The concept of the group dynamic must be incorporated into the selection and integration process. When choosing lures, you must view lure selection from the perspective of the fish. Detach yourself from the world above the waves and try and imagine what the lures look like, through the eyes of the fish, within their environment. This requires three-dimensional thinking. As you select lures, try to view or understand what individual lures look like as they are trailing a lead core, or a downrigger or a Dipsy at the target level. Imagine what each individual lure looks like in combination with the other lures in your spread.

Remember, your individual lines are not running in a vacuum. Each individual bait is part of a collective, the group dynamic. If you think of your lures and delivery devices this way, it will help you better understand their performance. Also, remember the exact line up locations where individual lures perform best. Keep a log to help you remember these important details. This will help you to pick productive lures every time you go fishing.

Principle 5: Read the Water

The fifth principle of lure selection is your ability to read the water and conditions and then factor in a dozen or more variables that impact how a lure appears from the perspective of a hungry chinook salmon. Selecting the right lure to consistently catch Oncorhyuchus Tshawytscha is a process that appears complicated, but once you begin choosing lures within this methodology, it becomes second nature.

In *Great Lakes Salmon And Trout Fishing*, I isolated twelve variables that impact lure performance and selection as lure category, lure color, target species, target depth, trolling speed, season, size, delivery method, need of an attractor, sea conditions, local weather, and the compatibility factor or group dynamic. These variables are always at play. Whether you are conscious of them or not, they are impacting your trolling spread. Every time you choose a lure to run for kings, these variables should be run through your selection matrix.

Do you need to consciously think about these variables? At first, yes, but over time, you will internalize these variables and you will instinctively learn how to factor them into the decision making process. How to choose lures and attractors will be unpacked in Chapter 7.

THREE-DIMENSIONAL THINKING

The majority of anglers fishing on the Great Lakes use controlled depth fishing techniques to deliver lures to precise target depths. The concept of controlled depth fishing suggests that multiple layers of the water column are at play since you are inserting your lures into different locations within the water column. A major component of success is your ability to look at the water three-dimensionally. Once you put a lure on the line and it slips past the surface, that lure enters a different world. Unless you are running only one line, that lure will not be alone. Other lures will be *swimming* along with it. All the lures and delivery devices you are trolling will be arranged in relationship, one to another, horizontally and vertically.

Learning to choose lure colors based on target depth, makes for a great catch.

Understand this point before moving on. You have a choice: You can set lines and run each lure independently without giving any thought to the spacial relationships between baits. Or, you can control the spacial relationships and craft combinations or teams that form a holistic group dynamic. Even if you are not thinking about these spacial relationships, they exist beneath and behind your boat when you are trolling multiple numbers of lines. Those relationships, or lack of, will be impacting your fish catch whether you are aware of them or not. If you choose to control the spacial dynamics beneath your boat, you will attract more kings into your lure spread and you will catch more fish.

Three-dimensional thinking requires you to be systematic in your approach to selecting lures and setting lines. You must view your individual lures in relation to the other baits in the water. You must also selectively use a variety of delivery devices to deploy your lures. Ultimately, you will weave the lures, attractors and delivery devices into a cohesive lure spread. We will examine this in greater detail in Chapter 6; now, let's examine the impact of color on the lure selection process.

LURE COLOR: HOW TO PICK WINNING COLOR COMBINATIONS

Can Kings Distinguish Color?

We all know color selection is critical in persuading fishermen to buy lures, but does color play a significant role in triggering king strikes? Let's go a step further; can chinook salmon visually distinguish between individual colors?

I am not a biologist, but I have read some interesting articles discussing the visual capacities of fish. I do believe that kings, can at the very least, distinguish shades of colors. This makes color a variable that can influence kings into striking. Still have doubts? I've been chartering since the early '80's and have experienced way too many days where slight alterations in lure color made all the difference in the world. When I know kings are present but not striking, I will systematically change lure colors until I have the right color combination in the water. Color is a major variable impacting success.

The frequency of light waves varies with depth based on light penetration, water clarity and sea conditions. This texture of the water determines what every individual color patterns look like, from the perspective of the fish, at the target depth. Since the texture of the water changes from day to day and hour to hour, you will frequently have to change lure colors to keep hooking kings. Color does matter.

I feel better after getting that off my chest. Now, let's get down to business and put the meat and potatoes on the table—a little discussed fact among Great Lakes anglers is the impact of target depth on lure color. Top tournament anglers and Charter Captains use target depth to determine lure color.

Have you ever watched one of the nature shows on TV where a school of baitfish is being "balled up" and chased by salt-water predators? Do you remember the shimmering, dancing and darting look that the frightened baitfish displayed? Now, picture a school of alewives (or other bait fish) in the Great Lakes and try to imagine what their frenzied swimming action might look like 20 feet beneath the surface on a cloudy day? Fifty feet down on a sunny day? Sixty-five feet down on a cloudy day? Or, maybe 92 feet down on a sunny day? Get the picture? Schools of baitfish (and individual baitfish) will look different depending on water texture, target depth within the water column and light conditions.

Just as the baitfish will look different at various levels, so will your artificial offerings. Individual lures, attractors and delivery apparatus will look different as you change their vertical location within the water column. Every color and color combination will also appear different, from the fish's perspective, at various target depths. The individual patterns will also take on different looks as sea, sky and light conditions change. Therefore, a key concept to remember is that a school of alewives (or other bait fish) and your lures will look very different from one target depth to the next. If the appearance of the forage fish suddenly changes (from the perspective of the fish) then you might have to change lure colors to match the conditions beneath the waves. To catch kings you want to mimic or match the appearance of the natural prey kings are feeding on when you are fishing.

The application that follows is simple. Certain individual color patterns will be more productive at different levels. When I choose lure colors, the target depth at which the lure will be deployed is a major factor influencing color selection. Experienced anglers have learned to recognize which color patterns are productive 40 feet down and which patterns work better 90 feet down. When they want to change a lure that will be running 90 feet down, they will pick a pattern that is a proven winner at that level, not a pattern that works better at higher levels of the water column.

On every charter, my goal is for all lines to produce fish. If one lure is hot at 75 feet and I have a dead rod running through kings 40 feet down, chances are, I will need a different color to trigger strikes at 40 feet. When targeting different layers of the water column you will usually need to use different color patterns.

A brief word needs to be said about glow lures. Glow baits are as popular as ever and rightly so, kings love glow! You can find spoons, flies, dodgers, flashers and plugs that glow. Glow should be viewed as a separate color.

Some spoons feature surfaces that are painted glow and other spoons have glow stripes. Many of the best king spoons feature a glow stripe running at a diagonal slant across the non-glow colors painted on the face of the spoon. (The Green Dolphin, Blue Dolphin and Caramel Dolphin

Choosing Lure Colors Based On Target Depth	
0-30 Feet	Green, Red, Yellow, Gold
30-60 Feet	Aqua, Green, Red, Yellow, Glow, Silver
60-80 Feet	Aqua, Pearl/Blue, White, Green, Glow, Silver
80-100 Feet	Pearl/Blue, Aqua, White, Blue, Glow, Silver
100-150 Feet	Pearl, White, Blue, Pearl/Blue, Aqua, Silver

patterns are good examples) What impact does a glow stripe have on lures? Some have suggested the diagonal glow stripe enhances a spoon's action and makes the spoon look like a crippled alewife through a visual illusion created by the spoon's motion. Go back to the nature channel and think of a large school of bait and how bait shimmers—one minute it looks like one large fish, next it looks like many individual fish. Does a glow stripe have the same effect on an individual lure? Does a glow stripe make a spoon look more life-like? Spoons with glow stripes are dynamite so this thought deserves attention.

While glow colors are highly productive during low light conditions

That's a king!

early and late in the day, and at night, they also work during bright mid day hours. When you are fishing murky or stained water, glow baits are also effective. Anytime you are fishing kings during low light hours, glow baits of some sort should be incorporated into your spread.

CHAPTER 6

The Group Dynamic And King Salmon: The Art Of Integration

After a long day out on the water, have you ever sat back and reflected on the events of the day? The decisions you made? The lures you chose? The mixture of delivery devices deployed? Did you take any risks? *What were the most important factors influencing success that day?* Was it being in the right location, three miles south of the harbor in 147 feet of water? Was it being *dialed in?* Was it a magic lure? Was it always a speed issue?

While all of the preceding factors are important, when viewed in isolation, these individual factors are incomplete. It is only when these elements are woven into a complete system that they reach their full potential. This complete system is what is known as the *group dynamic*.

In *Great Lakes Salmon And Trout Fishing*, I stressed the importance of collective thinking when it comes to picking lures and setting lines. Comprehensive thinking is the foundation of the *group dynamic*. Every time you troll with multiple lines in the water, you will create a group dynamic. Understanding the group dynamic and the interspatial distances between lures, delivery apparatuses and the boat are critical to success with king salmon.

HOW TO MAKE WISE CHOICES ON THE WATER

Let's be honest, fishing is a game of decisions. Every time you put a line in the water, you will be faced with a variety of choices. What direction should you motor to start fishing? How deep should you set your lines? Should you run two riggers or four? Should you run a wire Dipsy or a super line Dipsy? How close should you set one line to the next? Should you run two dodgers next to each other? Should you change your trolling angle?

Throughout the day, your success, or lack of success, will depend on the choices you make. What is your attitude toward the choices you face? Do you choose lures randomly or are you intentional in selecting and tracking lures? When setting lines, what determines your choice of delivery devices? Do you set your lines in a pattern, or do you just dump lines in the water and troll? Do you adjust your lines, or add or subtract different delivery devices? Is there any overall method to your madness, or do you just head out on the water and troll! How you approach these decisions (delivery devices, lure selection, setting lines and adjusting lines and trolling speed/angle) determines the effectiveness (or, for some, the ineffectiveness) of the group dynamic.

There are two general ways to approach this—you can randomly go through the motions of lure selection and placement or you can systematically factor in the variables that influence success and make wise decisions. The second method reaches its full potential when you build a comprehensive plan and execute your plan with intentionality.

If you want to maximize your fishing effort, you need to think collectively. You are not running an individual downrigger, a lead core, an individual Dipsy Diver, an individual wire line . . . you are running a team of lures. You utilize a variety of different delivery devices and techniques to place your carefully selected group of lures into the strike zone. Remember, the lures you are trolling are not running in a vacuum. Each individual lure and delivery device will impact (positively or negatively) the other baits in the water. The combined effect of your group dynamic will do one of two things: draw kings into our spread and trigger strikes or repel kings and not trigger strikes.

Every time you troll for kings, you will set out a new spread of baits and delivery devices. In essence, you create a new group dynamic every time you go fishing. Obviously you will follow general patterns, such as using four riggers, two Dipsies, a lead core and a suspended wire, but each new day will require you to adjust the dynamics and inter spatial distances of your lines within the dynamic.

I refer to this crafting element as the *texture* of the group dynamic. When choosing a piece of sandpaper for a wood project, the texture of the sandpaper you choose will determine how hard you have to work to

Learning to make wise decisions on the water will lead to fish like this.

finish the job. The texture, the spatial distances between your trolling devices and lures, influences success.

A wide range of variables impacts the texture of every individual group dynamic. These variables can be classified as direct and indirect variables. The direct variables are the ones you control. These include choice of delivery devices, line type (mono, wire, super braid, lead core, copper), lure selection (includes group, brand, color and size), water depth being fished, depth targeted, use of attractors, trolling speed/angle, boat size and number of lines. The direct variables are the areas you tweak and adjust as you dial into the fish. Indirect variables are beyond your control and include season, weather, target species availability and temperament, sea conditions, currents and boat traffic.

Is all this important or is Captain Dan just babbling? Remember, when you troll for kings you have a choice; you can randomly throw a group of baits in the water, and wander around, fishing each line independently. Or, you can orchestrate your lines into a complete, dynamic system. Within the system, you will systematically choose lures and intentionally weave the lures and the delivery devices into a cohesive spread. This methodology requires greater concentration from you, but it will produce more and larger kings and result in fewer tangles.

INTEGRATION AND THE GROUP DYNAMIC

If you are still tracking with me, you've either bought into the concept of the group dynamic, or you are thinking about it. If the jury is still out, stick with me! Every time you chase kings, you need to think collectively. You are running a complete spread of baits, made up of multiple parts, moving through designated layers of the water column. As you set lines, you are weaving together a team of lures with a common goal—to draw kings into your spread and trigger strikes.

> How you weave your lures and delivery devices into a complete team will determine whether kings are drawn into your spread, or turned off.

When adjusting lines you need to ask how will each lure work with the other lures already in the water. As you send individual lures to the strike zone, you must seek the optimum combination of delivery devices. This combination may change from hour to hour. For example, will two downriggers, two wire Dipsies and two super line Dipsies be the best combination? Or should you deploy two lead cores, two downriggers and two super line divers? Should you run half dodgers and half clean spoons . . . or all flies and dodgers? Integration is all about reading the water and conditions, interpreting the mood of the fish, making choices and implementing those choices.

The more time spent fishing with a posture of collective thinking, the more you will learn the strengths and weaknesses of your lures and delivery teams. You will develop *teams* of lures that always produce well when run together under distinct seasonal weather and sea conditions. Remember, fishing success is often a matter of repeatability. You must read the conditions and duplicate successful responses to conditions XYZ. Catching boatloads of kings does not require you to reinvent the wheel every time you fish!

THREE-DIMENSIONAL THINKING: A THEORETICAL DISCUSSION ON BUILDING A STRIKE BOX

We live in a multi-dimensional world, yet many anglers go fishing with a one-dimensional mindset. Many do not fully comprehend the dimensions (space, depth and distance) of the world beneath the waves. Popular thinking leads us to believe that all fish are simply swimming around beneath the surface of the water. Our minds don't go much further than that.

Well, I would like to change that. My dear friend and long time fishing partner, Doc Rupprecht, used to call me "Ol' Chinook Brain." He used to joke that my parents had genes from the brain of a chinook fused into my brain during my youth. Joking aside, if you want to catch more kings, you need to think like a king salmon. How do you think like a fish? You begin by focusing your mind and strategy on the world beneath the waves. The methodology to building a productive group dynamic is to continually visualize what all the lures and delivery devices look like together from the perspective of Mr. Salmon. This requires you to view the strike zone vertically and horizontally. In other words, you need to think three-dimensionally.

To gain some traction on this thought, let's create boundaries (dimensions) to the layers of water beneath your boat. When you are setting lines think in terms of a *strike box*. The strike box is the target layers or zone(s) you are targeting. This will help you to focus your mind on the world where kings live.

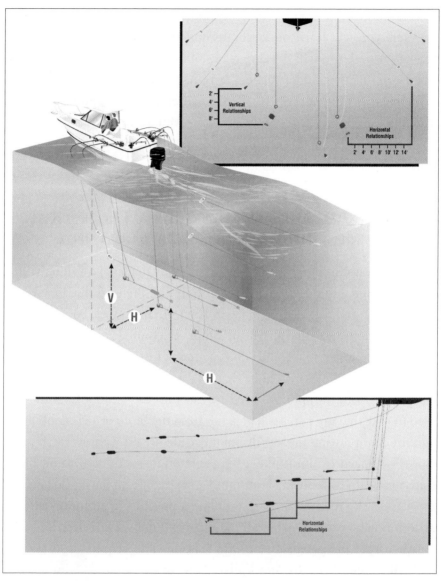

When setting lines you need to view the strike zone vertically and horizontally. These diagrams illustrate the vertical and horizontal relationships that form every group dynamic.

Let's step onto the baseball diamond for a moment to understand the importance of the strike box. Before a pitcher throws the first pitch, he must size up the batter and determine the parameters (boundaries) of the strike zone. This will determine *where* the pitcher needs to throw the ball.

Hitting the strike zone is critical for a Major League pitcher and requires constant adjustments by the pitcher. You see, the exact dimensions of the strike zone vary between players. Each individual player is a different height. A secondary element influences how a pitcher approaches the strike box. Every batter hits the ball differently; depending on where in the strike zone (or just outside the strike zone) the pitcher places the ball. The pitcher's job is to know the strengths and weakness of each player he will face. Then, he must execute by throwing the ball through the strike zone (or just outside or inside) at the player's weakest point. If a pitcher throws three strikes, the batters out. If the pitcher throws four balls outside the strike zone, the batter takes a base.

Trolling for kings is similar in that you want to hit the strike zone with your best pitch to trigger strikes. If a pitcher misses the strike zone repeatedly, he'll be pulled from the game. If you miss the strike zone when trolling, you will be eating chicken for dinner.

OK, I know after that little detour you want to go to Wrigley Field, but let's put the hot dogs and soda down and head back out on the water. Over the course of the fishing season, you will build a variety of strike boxes. Each individual strike box has vertical and horizontal dimensions. The dimensions will vary from day to day and depend on season, water stratification, fish location within the water column, rod selection and fish temperament.

Before you start dropping lines, you need to determine the vertical and horizontal boundaries of the *strike box*. The layers within the water column that you are targeting determine the vertical range. For example, you may be targeting a vertical range 10 feet deep one day and 50 feet deep another day. Water temperature, bottom structure, baitfish, current and king location are the key variables determining the vertical parameters.

The horizontal dimensions of the strike box need to be viewed three dimensionally. First, you have the horizontal boundary that extends at a 90-degree angle port and starboard from the center of your boat. Secondly, the horizontal layer extends linearly on a horizontal plain behind the boat (lead lengths). This secondary horizontal element is very important and often ignored. The two horizontal lines meld together and form an overall horizontal plane.

The vertical and horizontal dimensions of the strike box are ultimately determined by your choice of delivery devices and where you set them. *If you can grasp the horizontal and vertical dimensions created by controlled depth fishing you will gain control over the group dynamic.* If you have a plan before you start setting lines, you will more effectively target kings and have fewer tangles! People often just put a bunch of lines in the water and think everything is all neat and orderly beneath the waves. The ugly reality of multiple line tangles is a clear reminder that lines are not always where we think they are!

Remember, your lures and delivery devices are not running next to each other (linearly) in a perfectly horizontal line. When you troll multiple numbers of fishing lines, you will create a variety of horizontal and vertical relationships between individual lures. Lures and delivery devices play off one another and influence productivity. For example, two downriggers will have a horizontal and vertical relationship. The downrigger baits will also have horizontal and vertical relationships with any Dipsies that may be running outside them.

Macro Patterns to the Strike Box

As you fill your strike box with lures and delivery devices a macro pattern will govern the vertical dimensions of your line sets. The four most popular patterns are the V, inverted V, the M and the W pattern. The V pattern places your deepest lines directly beneath the boat. As you move away from the center, the vertical depth of lures rises up in the water column. The M pattern is my favorite. It takes the V concept and forms two legs by dropping one Dipsy on each side to the deepest corners of the strike box. The inverted V calls for running your boom riggers deep and your corners high. The W has your corner riggers deep, a lead core down the chute and your Dipsies are used to fish higher levels.

Building a Strike Box: Practical Application

When setting lines how do you determine the dimensions (broad or narrow) of a strike box targeting kings? Most people who fish for kings do not have the luxury of fishing every day of the week so you will be dealing with an element of mystery as you try to determine where and how to set your lines. If you follow the theoretical application of the strike box, you will quickly and efficiently dial into kings.

When targeting kings, the vertical and horizontal dimensions of your strike box are determined by seven key factors:

- Water temperature
- Target depth (this determines what delivery devices can be utilized)
- Fish temperament
- Baitfish location
- Time of day
- Season
- Weather

During the summer months water temp defines the vertical dimensions. Your primary target range is the 42 to 48-degree band of water. A secondary range extends up to the 54-degree layer. Begin the day by drawing an imaginary horizontal line through the level where the 42-degree water meets 41-degree water. This is the floor of your strike box. Next, set your ceiling at the 54-degree level. On bright days you may want to drop the ceiling down to the 48-degree layer once the sun hits the water. If action is slow and you have some additional rods to put in the water, you may want to expand the ceiling of the strike box up to the 58-degree layer. Typically, you will catch the largest kings in 42 to 44 degree water during mid-day. Under dark, heavy overcast, kings will rise higher up in the water column than on sunny days. When facing these conditions, you may want to set a higher limit on your strike box.

If you are fishing during the spring or late fall when ice cold water runs from the surface to the bottom, you cannot exclusively build a strike box based on water temperature. During cold water months, kings can be found anywhere in the water column. The vertical parameters are then determined by baitfish location, current, bottom structure and sonar readings.

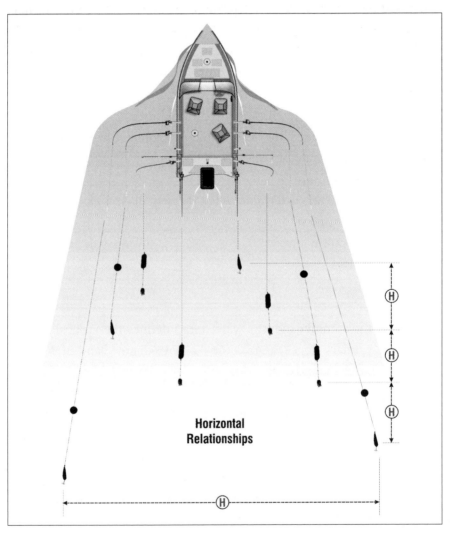

Many anglers ignore the horizontal relationships between delivery devices and lures. This diagram, looking down into the water, illustrates the two planes of horizontal separation inherent in the group dynamic.

Defining the horizontal dimensions of your strike box is an art form. The major influences on the horizontal dimensions are target depth (which is really a by-product of the vertical dimension), sea conditions and currents, fish temperament and your ability to deploy the various delivery devices available.

Which delivery devices to run is determined by the level targeted. You only want to run delivery devices that can reach the target depth. If the kings are 100 feet down, running four mono side planers and two mono Dipsies will not reach the fish.

Delivery devices, line application and lead lengths determine the horizontal breadth of your group dynamic. On the horizontal plane, there will be multiple horizontal relationships. The inner group dynamic is created by your downriggers. These lines are, for the most part, directly under your boat's path, and a few feet to the side (if you use boom riggers with pancake weights). Horizontally, the lures will trail behind the weights. Dipsy Divers will run further to the side of this inner group dynamic and add horizontal breadth to your lure group. Now, you can extend your range even further if you put lead core, super line with ball weights, wire line or copper out on side planers. Get the picture—you can create tight, narrow strike boxes or wide-open boxes by varying degrees.

To illustrate, let's build a theoretical strike box and focus on the vertical and horizontal elements. It's late summer and the kings are thick 75 to 110 feet down. This is the vertical range of this strike box and it covers 35 feet. Now, we need to determine the horizontal boundaries. First, you have your inner group dynamic. If your boat has a 10-foot beam and you have four foot booms on your outside riggers, you will have a horizontal breadth of about 16 to 18 feet (on a perpendicular angle from the center of the boat). Now, if you add pancake weights to the booms (in place of round weights), your boom riggers will run several feet further out to the side. You've just added horizontal distance, opening up your inner group dynamic to a width of 20 to 22 feet (depending on target depth, trolling speed and current).

You can add greater horizontal distance at the target depth by deploying one or two Dipsy Divers off each side. The horizontal breadth of the strike box is determined by line choice (mono, super, wire), Dipsy setting and target level. Since the kings are deep, let's run two wire divers on a 1½ setting. The horizontal boundaries created by the Dipsies (on a perpendicular range) are 10 to 15 feet to the side. The breadth of this group dynamic is about 45 to 50 feet. The horizontal range of this strike box will extend 120 feet behind the boat if we add a wire line tail gunner. The dimensions of this particular strike box are 35 feet deep, 50 feet wide and 120 feet long. All your lures are within that theoretical box.

Let's look at a second example, an early summer scenario where kings are suspending 30 to 70 feet down. The vertical dimensions are 40 feet. Since lead cores on side planers will be deployed the horizontal dimensions will extend out 100 feet to each side of the boat. The early summer strike box might also extend 100 yards behind your boat (horizontally) through the use of lead core. The area being covered by a full spread of lead cores, side planers, downriggers and Dipsies is huge! The dimensions of your strike box will vary over the course of the fishing season.

Fish temperament is the wild card of the group dynamic and is a major factor to consider when building a strike box. Kings are the moodiest, most temperamental salmonid in the Great Lakes. They are notorious for going on massive feeding frenzies and then getting lockjaw or disappearing for days at a time. I've often wondered if DNR biologists implanted a little switch on their noses that could be used to turn them on and off. *Minor adjustments to the spatial relationships within the group dynamic are often the solution to catching moody kings.*

What does this look like? When kings are aggressive, they may want the lures tightly packed into a narrow window. Spatially, you will want less distance between baits. Downriggers will be run on short leads, Dipsies will be set on 1-1½ settings to keep the diver close to the inner dynamic. The more commotion you create, the better. This concentrated commotion may be drawing fish into your spread and exciting them.

When kings are aggressive, dodgers and flashers are most productive. Early in the morning, tightly packed group dynamics are awesome.

Other times, you will need to spread your offerings out or actually reduce the number of lines in the strike zone to draw strikes. Riggers will be run on long leads, Dipsies set on 3 settings and lead, copper and wire will be applied. When kings are negative, I have found that less baits and delivery apparatuses in the strike zone will actually produce more strikes. On these days if you try to flood the strike zone with lures and delivery devices, you will catch few kings, even if you have 10 of the hottest baits in their face. Negative kings require a *skinny* or *sparse* group

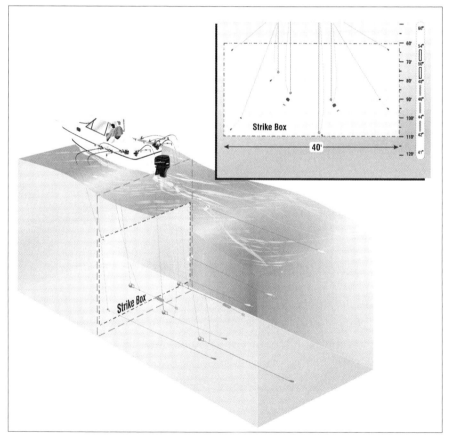

Hitting the strike zone with your best pitch is critical! When setting lines, think in terms of the strike box. This will help you to systematically zero in on big kings.

dynamic. During the mid-day, the skinny group dynamic will frequently produce more kings. A high percentage of clean spoons are the best baits for negative kings.

If large schools of baitfish are present, you should consider running lines at the level of the bait, even if the bait is out of the preferred temperature range. Kings will go out of temperature to grab an easy meal. For this reason, if you are targeting kings in cold water down 70 feet, but you mark a cloud of bait 40 feet down in 58-degree water, it might pay to run a line at the 40-foot level. When I am marking bait in the warmer layers of the water column, I like to put a super line Dipsy out on a $2\frac{1}{2}$ setting with a yellow Jensen Dodger and a double aqua Howie or Tournament Fly. This is a great snack for big kings in warm water.

Season, time of day, and weather will also impact the parameters of your group dynamic. Early and late in the day, kings will rise up in the water column. You will want to raise the ceiling of the strike box 10-30 feet higher in the water column early in the pre-dawn morning and again if you are fishing in the evening. Also, if a storm front moves in or a heavy chop and dark overcast develops, you may want to raise the upper limits of your strike box. Any sudden weather or sky change may require you to make minor adjustments to your strike box in order to catch kings. Kings are very weather and light sensitive.

RELATIONSHIPS WITHIN THE GROUP DYNAMIC

When you are targeting kings you are like a spider weaving a web. As you change lures, lead lengths, depths, speeds, angles and delivery devices, the combined effect of your choices will determine what your group dynamic looks like over the course of the day.

Once you have determined the vertical and horizontal boundaries of the strike box, you will want to think about the relationships within the box. The distance between the individual lures and delivery devices is as important as the lures themselves. Every line, delivery device, attractor and lure is impacting other elements within the spread. In other words, the right bait run in the wrong location on the wrong delivery apparatus will not catch kings.

I am going to repeat this: *individual lines are not running in a vacuum*. When you change a lure or delivery device, you need to consider how that change will impact the other lures in the water. Within each group dynamic, there may be smaller dynamics or combinations relating to one another. For example, a pair of Dipsies running side by side will almost function like a halfback following a fullback down the field.

It is often the impact or signature of the entire spread that attracts kings. You control the spread's impact by the way you set the lines. For example, the distance you set your lures behind downrigger weights impacts success. I set my rigger lead lengths in a pattern. If kings are high and skittish, all leads will be long. If kings are aggressive and holding at mid or deep levels, I will stagger the leads. I may run two riggers on short leads (5 to 20 feet) to draw kings in and run the remaining riggers long. The combined effect of your choices will determine what your group dynamic looks like over the course of the day. This combined effect is one of the most important aspects of trolling for kings.

This catch of summer kings was made on an integrated spread of clean spoons, flies, dodgers and flashers.

When you start popping kings, re-set your lines exactly the same! If a downrigger with a 40-foot lead takes a big guy down 64 feet, boat the fish and set the lure in exactly the same location! Don't change it by an inch. To do this, you need to pay attention to details when you are setting lines! Also, the lines surrounding a hot pole may have as much to do with the success of an individual lure. For this reason, you may need to duplicate all the lures around a hot bait. If one rod is on fire and you change an adjacent rod(the lure running next to it in the water) and the hot rod dies, you may have to put the original lure back on the rod just changed. This happens frequently when fishing dodgers and flashers, as the dodgers and flashers frequently draw fish into a spread of baits.

Pattern Fishing

When you walk the docks of the local charter fleet, you will find some captains who advocate what is called *pattern fishing*. Pattern fishing is where you put out a spread of lures that are identical. Some very good Captains will put the same color flasher and fly on every line. Port Washington, Wisconsin, Captains like to load the water with yellow Coyotes

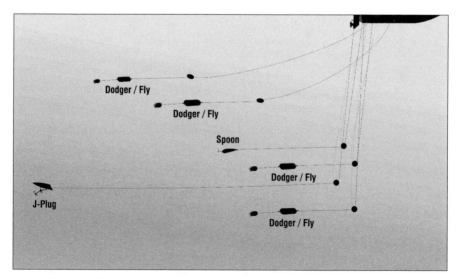

The Odd Ball Effect is a deadly tactic for stubborn kings. Often, the one lure that looks out of place will take the biggest fish.

with lead and silver tape with a double aqua Howie Fly. Some may put the exact same spoon (type, size and color) on every line. The philosophy behind this method is that you are trying to imitate a school of alewives. It is a method that you may want to incorporate into your game plan.

I have a unique spin to pattern fishing and I call it the *Odd Ball Effect*. While I do not typically pattern fish, in the strict sense that all the lures are identical, I will occasionally run a heavy spread of assorted colors or brands of dodgers, flashers and flies. When I do this, I like to keep at least one clean spoon in the pack. This different lure, the oddball, often takes the largest kings. A number 4 J-Plug is another great oddball bait.

Confusion within Selection

When you are fishing, be cautious of the endless stream of new lures. If you have too many lure choices you can become easily confused. This can actually lead you to less fish! I met one angler at an outdoor show during the winter that confessed that he needed to take several boxes of spoons off his boat. He had too many lures to choose from, and at times, he had junk on his lines because he had lost sight of what he was look-ing for! Having excessive variety does not allow you to focus on your gear. Learn how to fish a manageable selection of good baits well.

When fishing gets tough, some anglers will change all the good baits and patterns and end up with a *Far Side* line up of lures. When the fish turn on, or they find kings, they don't capitalize on the bite because they are trolling with second tier lures. When I am hunting for kings, I will keep my best baits in the water and restrict the urge to constantly change lures. If I know kings are present, but I am not getting strikes, I will sys-tematically change baits. When changing lures I leave my best baits on key rods and designate several rods as experimental. I will systematically begin changing lures on these rods every 10 to 15 minutes, looking for a pattern.

Michael Jordan was not alone when the Chicago Bulls took to the court. Your lures are not alone. When your lures and delivery devices function as a team, rather than individually, you will catch way more kings than you ever dreamed. With experience you will learn the strengths and weaknesses of your lures and delivery devices. You will develop *teams* of lures and you will recognize the conditions those teams score under. Remember, repeatability is a huge part of success when trolling for King Salmon. You do not need to reinvent the wheel every day. Great success comes to those who learn to isolate conditions and then can duplicate successful patterns when they face similar conditions.

The Odd Ball Effect of a lone J-Plug in a spread of spoons and flies was too much for this king to pass up.

CHAPTER 7

How To Pick Winning King Baits Every Day

Why do some lures catch more kings than others? What makes one lure more attractive to kings than another? Let's begin with the basics. Chinook baits can be divided into three categories: spoons, body baits and flies, dodgers and flashers. Is one lure group more effective than the others? This is a loaded question and for one angler, spoons may butter the bread and for another, it may be flies and flashers or plugs that carry the mail. The purpose of this chapter is to equip you with the tools required to make wise choices on your home waters. While lists of hot lures are great, you will catch more and larger kings if you learn to read the water, analyze conditions and choose the right combination of lures to meet the current conditions.

Can you rely on only one type of lure, such as flies and dodgers? As you know, weather conditions, seasons and fish temperaments vary greatly from one month to the next. To respond to the ever-changing conditions, you should learn to use lures from all three categories.

Before moving on, please understand that all lures have their strengths and weaknesses. Within each category, certain individual baits are more productive. Don't limit yourself to thinking that you have to run exclusive spreads of spoons or flies. Every day, a different combination of baits will draw maximum strikes. When I am targeting kings, I like to run integrated lure spreads that will incorporate baits from two or three lure groups. There are some anglers, though, who believe in pattern fishing. Pattern fishing involves running baits from only one lure group. In this chapter, I will unpack the distinguishing features of the three lure groups.

The term 'clean lure' will be used frequently. A clean lure is one that is run without an attractor. Spoons and plugs are typically run clean.

Attractors can be divided into two categories: direct and indirect. Direct attractors are the devices, such as dodgers or cowbells that are tied directly into the fishing line. Their primary purpose is to impart action and attract fish to the trailing lure. Most people are aware of direct attractors.

Indirect attractors are multi-dimensional and often ignored. When chasing kings with controlled depth fishing tactics, Dipsy Divers and downrigger weights function as indirect attractors. They impart additional action to a lure through oscillation and boat movement. They are visual stimulants and can *audibly* enhance or detract the signature of the group dynamic. Both direct and indirect attractors impact more than just the trailing bait—they impact the entire group dynamic. Each individual attractor will impact every other lure in your entire lure spread or group dynamic.

FLIES, DODGERS AND FLASHERS: THE FRONT LINE OF TODAY'S CHINOOK TROLLING OFFENSIVE

Flies, dodgers and flashers revolutionized the way we fish for chinooks on the Great Lakes. In the late 70's and early 80's, we caught loads of big fish, but we did it with spoons, plugs and squids and metal dodgers. In my home region, an enterprising engineer named Howard Halsne, started tying these goofy looking tinsel things. I remember the grin on Howie's face as he would walk down the dock, passing out his flies. Several of us, Jeff Heinz, Arnie Arredondo, Mike Smith, Jerry Neid and myself to name a few, began using these early flies with great success. Some of Howard's creations were as effective as a stick of dynamite! To tighten up a long story, Howard changed the way we fish. In the grind of charter fishing, Howard's flies out-produced all other lures, under a variety of conditions. Since those early days, other people have introduced a variety of flashers and dodgers to the market that have continued to improve the productivity of the dodger, flasher and fly system.

Flies, dodgers and flashers are a system. A system is a group of parts, that when *properly* combined, form a complete entity. To effectively fish dodgers, flashers and flies, you must view them as a complete system— a team. Together, the team forms a complete picture. If you truly understand the parts and components of flies, dodgers and flashers, you will be able to use them to their full potential.

Stay with me for a minute before you move to the next section. Flies, dodgers and flashers are some of the deadliest baits for kings, but they are more difficult to use than spoons or cranks. They require more adjustment, tuning and attention. When properly run, however, they are

Properly tuned flashers and flies are excellent baits for trophy kings, as Captain Ernie Lantiegne (right) demonstrates.

one of the most productive lure systems available to catch king salmon. In fact commercial fishermen on the Pacific Coast have relied on flashers and dodgers for ages.

Before unpacking this far ranging topic, let's define the players and their functions. Flies are the final component in the equation. A single fly is comprised of the fly body (tinsel), a hook and a group of beads, floats or tubes. The most productive flies are between 3 and 4 inches long. Occasionally, longer flies up to 6 inches are used, as are shorter flies down to 1 inch. Tinsel is the most popular fly material. While hair flies are great for coho, the tinsel models will produce more kings.

Beneath the fly body anglers place two to five beads, Lindy Floats or a tube on the leader. While the utilitarian purpose of these is to keep the hook at the back end of the fly, savvy anglers have noticed that the productivity of an individual fly is greatly enhanced by the combination of colored beads or floats beneath the actual fly. The end of the leader is tied to a # 2 or # 1 treble hook. I like to use short shank trebles.

Does bead color really matter? YES! When you look at a fly, you need to think in terms of fly color and bead color. They are a team. When you put a fly in the water, its actual appearance depends on the color of beads beneath the tinsel. For this reason, a pearl blue fly with green beads will look different than the same pearl blue fly with yellow or blue beads. As an individual fly catches fish and disintegrates, bead color makes an even greater impact.

Let me illustrate this concept. One summer, pearl Howie flies with yellow beads were dynamite. If you put a pearl Howie with green beads out, you would catch plenty of coho, but not kings. One particular July day green crinkle Howie flies with four green beads were the ticket. The next day, a green crinkle Howie with black beads out-produced the green crinkle with green beads. If you just pulled your green crinkles with the green beads, you would have missed the best action. Some days simply changing bead color will trigger kings to strike. Kings are very selective and I can't over emphasize this enough!

While the actual fly body is critical, a trolled fly without a dodger will catch few kings by itself. A good analogy is an NFL fullback. If the fullback is by himself on the field, he won't score any touchdowns. He needs an offensive line to block and a quarterback to hand off the ball. For flies to catch fish, they need help. If the fly is going to draw strikes from kings, a dodger or flasher needs to give the fly action . . . and draw the attention of the fish.

Dodgers and flashers are multi-dimensional tools. While their primary purpose is to impart lure action to a lifeless fly, they fill several other important roles. They are a visual attractor as kings can see them and they give off vibrations that can be sensed by the lateral line nervous system of kings. When kings go deep, the vibration factor can be a major element in drawing kings into a spread of baits. Vibration also excites salmon and can help trigger strikes. Based on the sight appeal and audible (vibration) attraction of dodgers, they impact your entire group dynamic, not just the individual trailing fly.

Flies, dodgers and flashers are a system. A critical part of the system is the leader connecting the fly to the dodger. Leader length is as important as the fly and the flasher. Actual leader length will vary depending on size of attractor and the mood of the fish. Generally speaking, a 15 to 37-inch leader is used. Typically I like to use a 21 to 25-inch leader. I use 40 lb. test Ande mono, but fluorocarbon will also work.

Selecting Flies for King Salmon

What makes a big king smash one fly but pass up another? All flies are not created equal. Most anglers look at a collection of flies and think they are all the same. Your eye may lead you to that conclusion, but salmon can detect subtle differences between individual flies, brands and colors.

What are the differences? Color and size are obvious, but beyond that it comes down to construction and how a fly *disintegrates* once it has been put into use and caught fish. For example, a pearl/blue fly from one manufacturer may look slightly different when it's run through the water than a pearl/blue fly from a different company. The difference is chiefly in how the tinsel is cut (dimensions), the density of the completed fly and subtle color differences between tinsel types.

How a fly *disintegrates* once it is used also impacts presentation. Take a new fly, fresh out of the package and lay it next to the same brand and color fly that has caught 5 fish and one that has caught 20 fish. See the difference? The more fish an individual fly catches, the more its characteristics change or disintegrate. That is the nature of tinsel flies; they become thinner and more ragged with success.

I will let you in on a secret, pay attention. *Well-worn flies are better king flies than bulky, new flies.* Do you understand? As a fly wears, often they become irresistible to big kings. Save old flies and put them in a special box. When you are trying to *match the hatch,* these old flies will come in handy.

Matching a hot pattern is multi-dimensional and critical to success. It involves more than just color and brand. For example, if you have a double aqua Howie fly that is red hot on a Dipsy, you might want to put out a second double aqua Howie on a different rod. Look closely at the hot fly. What color beads does it have? Put it in the water boat side and

Big kings are selective! Notice the difference in texture between a new fly and a well-worn fly?

watch how it looks or shimmers when moved by the dodger. What is the flies density and length—if it has caught a lot of fish, it may be thinner and shorter. Kings can detect very minor differences in your lures. Remember, kings often strike out of reflex. They react to minor subtleties. *It is often the small adjustments that fill the cooler.*

Kings definitely favor certain fly colors. The target level of the water column should guide your decision when choosing fly color. When kings are in the top 30 feet, shades of green and aqua dominate. The 30 to 70-foot range is strong for aqua, crinkle green, green, green w/pearl blue and pearl blue. When kings go deeper than 70 feet white, pearl and pearl blue are the hottest colors. Aqua is the one fly color that consistently works across all depth levels.

Sky conditions can impact color selection. On foggy days, kings suspending between 40 to 90 feet down are suckers for powder blue flies. On dark, dreary days, the whites and pearl shades will work higher up in the water column. On bright days green shades will work down to 100 feet.

Kings are moody, so don't be afraid to experiment. Even slight changes in sky or sea conditions can impact fly selection. For example, you may have a strong bite with aqua flies and silver glow dodgers and all of a sudden the action stops. You're still marking fish, but you have not had a hit in 30 minutes. The clouds may have thinned out and the light penetration increased. The fly and dodger combo no longer looks appealing under the new conditions. On this particular day, you may have to replace your aqua and smoke combo with a green fly and a yellow flasher to keep the bite going. Remember, it is often the small observations and adjustments that make the difference.

Houston, We Have A Problem: Too Many Dodgers and Flashers to Choose From

Remember when life was simple . . . you used to go down to the local pond and toss a worm into the water and wait patiently for the bobber to disappear? As you grew older you began chasing bass and walleye and your targets got larger and larger. Then you ventured out onto one of the Great Lakes and caught your first king salmon. At that moment, it was all over. After that first run you were hooked. It was only a matter of time before you bought a boat and started acquiring salmon tackle.

If you began salmon fishing more than 10 years ago, lure selection was limited. Life remained simple. But the creative engineers of our beloved sport put an end to simplicity. What happened? As we learned more and more about catching salmon, new types and styles of dodgers and flashers were introduced. Today, you can fill a small boat with dodgers and flashers if you have an unlimited budget! I feel sorry for newbies to the sport of salmon fishing—how do you know *which* dodgers or flashers to use? How do you determine the right piece of metal or plastic for the job?

Well, whenever life gets confusing, I like to go back to the basics. The purpose of a flasher/dodger is threefold. They impart action to the trailing fly, visually attract fish and are a sound stimulant. These three characteristics (action, sight and sound) should determine which dodger or flasher you use. Most anglers focus on color and ignore the other

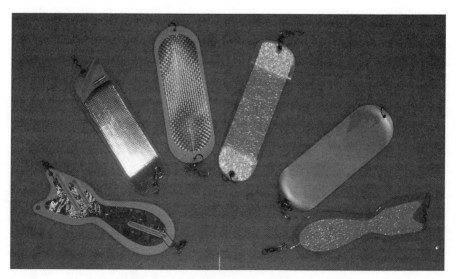

Dodgers and flashers come in a variety of shapes, sizes and colors. Learn to use them to your advantage!

aspects. For Great Lakes kings, the 8-inch size is most productive. Some anglers use the larger 11-inch variety, but these make boating hooked fish more difficult and don't work any better than the 8-inch variety.

I used to think one style or dodger brand fit all days. That all ended one calm July day after Shawn Kuelen of the *Breezy 1* taught me a valuable lesson on catching kings. Unfortunately, that classroom happened to be right under the bow of my boat and I was the student! I was struggling to catch fish. I had the occasional strike from a king or coho, but every time I talked to Shawn, he had just boated a double or a triple. We were fishing the exact same water. Our boats were making nearly identical passes over the fish, but I could not catch fish at the rate Shawn was. I returned to the dock with 8 fish and Shawn ended up with close to 20 nice kings. After cleaning the catch, I went over to Shawn's boat and looked at his rigs—one major difference almost knocked me off the dock—the dodgers that were on the four rods Shawn used to catch most of his fish. On that fine July morning, the major difference between Shawn's lure spread and mine was the brand of dodgers we were using. Shawn's catch made me feel like I needed to take up a new profession. Does the type or brand of dodger or flasher you are using make a difference—absolutely!

Let's talk action. The distinguishing feature that separates metal dodgers from plastic flashers (rotators) is their respective action. An ideal dodger action is a side-to-side swishing action with the occasional spin or flip thrown in. As you add speed, a dodger will cease the swishing and start to spin. Do dodgers catch fish at a full spin? Sometimes. Don't be afraid to spin your dodgers but keep in mind that dodgers are speed sensitive and require the angler to adjust their speed perfectly to achieve fish catching action.

Flashers, or rotators as Michigan anglers refer to them, have a very different and more predictable action than dodgers. Their trademark action is to swing in a wide symmetric circle with little or no erratic action. Some flashers have such predictable action that they will keep making the same, sweeping arc. Some brands, such as the Pro Chip 8, will display the occasional twist or swish within their arc pattern.

Flashers are more speed tolerant than dodgers. Many brands display the same rotating action across a broad spectrum of speeds. If you have a light weight boat or struggle with trolling speed, fish in rough water or strong currents, flashers are the logical choice. When using plastic flashers you don't have to dial your trolling speed in as precisely as with metal dodgers. In fact, some flashers, such as the Spin Doctor, will work at speeds as high as 3.2 kts.

A key variable to remember when differentiating between brands is their respective action. Individual brands behave differently when you pull them through the water. This results in a different action being imparted to the trailing fly and a different vibration signature.

Since the primary purpose of a dodger or flasher is to impart action to the fly, you should pay attention to what the fly is doing behind the blade. This is critical! When you run a dodger, the fly being pulled will display a much more erratic action as it darts around behind the dodger. When pulling flashers, the fly follows the same, predictable symmetric circle behind the flasher.

This fact was crystallized when I viewed Carl Stafinski's underwater video. Carl's underwater camera verified how different a fly could look from one attractor to another. What was more interesting was how kings approached these flies. Some fish swam up, quasi interested looked at the fly, and departed. Some fish followed the fly for great distances, curious but not buying. Other fish came in lit up and excited. These fish smashed the fly! Sometimes, kings will want the erratic action produced by a dodger. Other days, the symmetrical action imparted by a flasher will trigger strikes.

Next, let's examine the construction of dodgers and flashers. Dodgers are a flat piece of metal with slight cupping angles at each end. Flashers come in metal and plastic varieties. For chinooks the plastic variety are favored. Plastic flashers are light in weight and place less drag on tackle. Flashers also come in a variety of shapes. Some, such as Hot Spots, Pro Chips and Coyotes, are flat with sharply angled ends. Pro Chip also makes a flasher with angled ends but adds a fin to one end. This small fin gives it a slightly more erratic action. Some flashers, such as the Spin Doctors and Becholds, are flat with fins. Spin Doctors are shaped like a fish.

Vibration or sound (signature) is a secondary function of dodgers and flashers. The shape, construction and weight of the attractor influence the vibration or signature produced as the blade moves through the water. Most anglers don't factor this into their selection matrix. A metal dodger, swishing along, will *sound* very different to the lateral line of a feeding chinook than a light, plastic flasher rotating through the water. The Pro Chip 8 has a small E chip on the flasher. Theoretically, this emits a small impulse of electricity that the manufacturer claims attracts salmon.

Spin Doctors and Howies are a deadly combination for kings.

Does the brand of dodger or flasher make a difference, or are they all alike? Is there a difference between a Mercedes and a Saturn? Yes, brand matters. Now, some individual models are closer in action but there are subtle differences in the action imparted by the various brands. For kings, the most productive metal dodgers are the Luhr Jensen Dodger and the Opti Dodger. The Jensen dodger works better at slow speeds. Popular plastic flashers for kings include Hot Spots, Spin Doctors, Becholds, Pro Chips and Coyotes.

Dodgers and flashers also function as visual stimulants. This makes color a key component. I use target depth and fish temperament to determine blade color. For kings in the top 30 feet red and yellow dodgers get the nod. When kings are 30 to 70 feet down yellow (chartreuse) with yellow tape, yellow with silver or lead tape, silver glow and green are favored. When kings are 70 feet or deeper, silver glow, white, pearl, white/blue and silver are the most productive colors. For way deep kings 100 feet and deeper, white, silver glow and pearl blades are favored.

Attractor colors will look different (to the fish) depending on the *swishing* or *rotating* action of the dodger or flasher. From the fish's perspective, they see the dodger or flasher as it is *moving* through the water.

Top 10 Flies, Dodgers and Flashers for Kings Above 60 feet
Yellow (yellow tape) Jensen Dodger Double Aqua Howie
Chartreuse Hot Spot (glow/lead tape) Double Aqua Howie
Yellow (silver tape) Jensen Dodger Crinkle Green Howie
Smoke Jensen Dodger Glitter Aqua Howie
White Hot Spot Double Aqua Howie
White Spin Doctor (yellow tape) Crinkle Green Howie
Yellow Jensen Dodger Tournament Howie
Blue Bubble Spin Doctor Glitter Aqua Howie
White Hot Spot (lead/glow tape) Pearl Blue Howie
Red Jensen Dodger Aqua Howie

Top 10 Flies, Dodgers and Flashers for Kings Below 60 Feet
Blue Bubble Spin Doctor White Howie
Smoke Jensen Dodger Pearl Blue Howie
Blue Bubble Spin Doctor Double Aqua Howie
White Jensen Dodger Pearl Howie
White Hot Spot (lead/glow tape) White Howie
White Hot Spot (lead/glow tape) Double Aqua Howie
Chartreuse Hot Spot (lead/glow tape) Tournament Howie
Silver Jensen Dodger Pearl Blue Howie
White Hot Spot Pearl Blue Howie
White Pro Chip Pearl Blue Howie

They see the visual impact that the motion and the color of the blade produce. You and I see a piece of colored metal or plastic lying motionless on the deck.

Integrating Flies, Dodgers and Flashers into Your Trolling Spread

The key to catching kings on dodgers, flashers and flies is *how* and *where* you run them. You must pay attention to DETAILS when running a spread of dodgers or flashers. First, you need to match the right color fly with the right dodger color. A dodger and fly are a team. You will notice that certain *teams* will always produce kings and other teams will only produce lake trout or coho. When I come across a hot combination, say a white Howie with a blue bubble Spin Doctor, I will keep that team together. Some of my favorite king combos include double aqua Howie with a white Hot Spot with lead and glow tape, aqua glitter with yellow/yellow tape Jensen Dodger, green crinkle with silver glow dodger, double aqua with silver glow dodger, crinkle green/pearl blue with yellow flasher with lead and glow tape, aqua glitter with white flasher, pearl blue with silver glow, pearl with white dodger or flasher, white with white flasher or dodger and green crinkle with yellow dodger/silver tape.

At times I will have a team that is so hot, I will keep the individual fly with the dodger—I won't separate them because I don't want to lose track of the combo. When that team is not in use, it is stored separately (with the fly wrapped around the flasher), so it can be easily accessed when similar conditions arise. A box designed for storing flashers/dodgers is great for storing these hot rigs.

Next, focus on leader length. Travel across the Great Lakes and one charter captain will tell you leader length doesn't matter and the next captain will tell you it's the most important detail of the day. I believe leader length is imperative to catching kings. Leader length determines the amount of action (snap) that a fly exhibits. A shorter leader will impart more action to the fly and a longer leader will diminish the fly's action. When using the standard 8 to 9-inch dodger, a general leader range is 15 to 37 inches. Wasn't that a big help! Most days a 21 to 25-inch leader gets the call.

Every day is different, however, and you will have to determine the exact length each day. If the fish are aggressive, a shorter leader tends to draw more strikes. When kings go off the feed and become moody, a long lead of 28 to 37 inches will draw strikes. During the mid day doldrums a 27 to 34 inch lead may draw strikes. If the lake is flat calm or early in the morning, short leads of 19 to 23 inches work best.

Dodgers, flashers and flies produce tons of kings off all delivery applications. They can be mixed and matched with other baits or run exclusively. Lead length off the various delivery devices is critical. When running blades on Dipsies for kings I like a 7 to 9-foot leader. Six to eight foot leaders are used with suspended wire sinker drops. Metal dodgers and plastic flashers work equally well on divers and ball weights. For lead core fishing, I like the plastic flashers. For copper and wire flat lines, metal and plastic both work.

How far back do you run dodgers and flashers on downriggers? That depends on brand, target level, fish temperament and the group dynamic. Generally speaking, chinooks prefer a longer lead off riggers than coho, lake trout or steelhead. Also, the deeper you go in the water

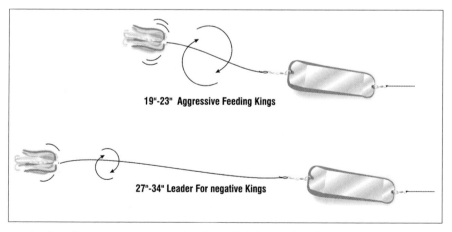

19"-23" Aggressive Feeding Kings

27"-34" Leader For negative Kings

Leader length is as important as the fly and dodger! This diagram illustrates how shorter leaders will impart more action to the fly.

column, the closer you want to run a dodger or flasher to the weight. When fishing 100 feet or more deep, 5 to 18 foot leads are standard. From 70 to 100 feet down try 8 to 30 foot leads. At the 40 to 70 foot level, leads of 10 to 40 feet are recommended. Above 40 foot, go with 10 to 50 foot leads. Metal dodgers, such as the Jensen dodger and the Opti, tend to work better on shorter leads of 8 to 15 feet. The Spin Doctor doesn't work off downriggers unless it is at least 20 feet back. In general, the plastic flashers will work better on longer leads than metal dodgers.

If your lead cores are red hot but your riggers are slow, try running a flasher and fly back 100 to 200 feet. When running super long leads off riggers with flashers or dodgers, be careful on your turns. On long leads they will wander and easily tangle other lines and sink down and snag zebra mussels off the bottom.

Where within the group dynamic you run a fly and dodger is just as important as the fly, dodger or flasher you use. Also, the percentage of dodgers or flashers to clean baits will influence success. Some days, all blades will be best. Other days, a few blades in a spread of clean spoons will trigger maximum action. This ratio changes from day to day, so be open-minded as you set lines. Also, the spacing between individual blades and clean baits is very important. Pay attention to how you set each line and where each lure and attractor is, in relation to the other lures in the water.

Dodgers, flashers and flies are a potent weapon in the arsenal of any angler who takes the time to learn how to run them. The key to success with running flies and dodgers is fine tuning your presentation and learning how to mix dodgers and flashers with other baits. They really are the linemen of the group dynamic and, when run properly, they will help you catch more kings!

SPOONS: USER FRIENDLY LURES

Spoons are a major player when it comes to catching Great Lakes chinooks. In some regions, they are the lure of choice. Spoons offer you an element of versatility that you don't find with crank baits or flies. They are easy to run because they track straight, work well in all locations within the group dynamic, tolerate strong currents and they are easily mixed and matched with a spread of flies/dodgers or cranks. Many of today's favorite salmon spoons are highly speed tolerant. You will not find this versatility with flies and cranks. Spoons produce kings at all levels from the surface to the bottom all season.

If you are fishing a spread of flies and dodgers and experience excess tangles, you may want to switch to spoons. When you encounter a strong current or are experiencing heavy side slipping, you should think about running spoons. With plugs and dodgers trolling speed has to be pegged exactly. Even if your speed is slightly off, many spoon brands, such as Silver Streaks, Dreamweavers, Grizzlies and Michigan Stingers will maintain fish catching action.

Trophy brown trout often strike clean spoons intended for kings.

While spoons can be run off all delivery devices they are most effective when used in conjunction with light line and downriggers. The key to this program is 12 lb. test line (or lighter) and a small, high quality ball bearing swivel. When spoon fishing off downriggers, the light line and small swivel allow a spoon to achieve maximum action. The light line also has minimal visibility compared to heavier test line. These two factors are hugely important in the super clear water found in the Great Lakes. An in depth discussion on spoons, light line and downriggers can be found in Chapter 8.

Spoon Fundamentals: Selection and Rigging

If you've walked into a tackle store recently you understand why the greatest challenge facing anglers is selection. Selection can be overwhelming! While endless choices may be part of living in postmodern America, you need to go back to the basics. If you have too many spoons to choose from, you will become disoriented and confused, right Bob?

To reduce the spoon world to a manageable size, focus on five selection criterions: size (length), weight, brand, delivery application and color pattern. This will help you to organize your thoughts, track winning baits and ultimately, catch more kings.

People who rely on spoons to catch chinooks know how to *match the hatch*. Spoon size is critical! Many days, spoon size, not brand or color is the determining factor in drawing strikes. For instance, frequently I will pull a regular size Silver Streak, Green Dolphin off a downrigger and put out a magnum Green Dolphin Streak. Guess what? I can't keep the magnum spoon (same color and brand) in the water. For the prior 30 minutes the same school of kings completely ignored the standard size Streak but they are all over the magnum spoon. If I didn't switch to a larger spoon, I would not have caught those kings!

I believe kings are more sensitive to lure size than the other salmonids found in the Great Lakes. Why? I think it has to do with the bait size kings are foraging. When small young of the year alewives and perch are present, the shorter spoons work best. When large alewives are abundant, the magnum spoons will out produce the smaller spoons by a wide margin. At times when fishing open water, I believe the larger spoons are easier for the kings to spot from greater distances. When kings are inshore prior to spawning, larger spoons often trigger their aggressive nature that a smaller spoon won't ping.

Most spoons come in three to five sizes. The magnum sizes are the largest and they are four to five inches long, depending on brand. The standard or "regular" size is 3 to 4 inches and mini spoons run 1½ to 2 inches in length.

Does an overall size pattern govern spoon fishing? While I wish I could give you a black and white rule to follow, I am afraid that I must offer a more ambivalent answer. On any given day, you must experiment with size. Even when you run charters every day, the hot size from Tuesday may not work on Wednesday. It is a rare day that I don't use spoons of at least two or three different sizes.

One size pattern governs late August and September. Large schools of small alewives, less than 1½ inches, dominate offshore kings diets.

Anglers use five sizes of spoons to match the hatch.

When this occurs, smaller spoons such as the Michigan Stinger, Grizzlies and mini Streaks are deadly baits. When warm water forces kings super deep (beyond 100 feet), they often feed on large adult alewives. Magnum spoons are strong performers under this scenario.

Chinook spoons can be organized by weight: light, medium and heavy. The medium weight spoons are the most productive for kings. These spoons maintain enticing, fish catching action over a broad range of speeds. These mid weight spoons can easily be mixed and matched with more speed sensitive baits such as dodgers and flies. Light spoons require ultra-slow trolling speeds and heavy spoons only work at faster speeds. If you use medium weight spoons with light line, you can troll over a broad range of speeds (1.5 to 3.2 Kts.) without having to change lures. I highly recommend that you use these mid-weight spoons when chasing kings.

Organizing spoons by brand is the third factor. While many brands may look similar in size, shape, weight and color, they will display subtle differences when trolled. This is where experience and good info come in handy. You need to learn which brands work best under different conditions on your home waters. The most productive king spoons across the Great Lakes are Silver Streaks, Dreamweavers, Michigan Stingers, Grizzlies, Maulers, Diamond Kings, Yuks, Fishlanders and Northern Kings.

Line up location (delivery application) is something many anglers ignore when selecting spoons. Just because one individual spoon (brand, size, color pattern) produces kings off downriggers doesn't mean it will catch kings off lead cores. On the *BLUE HORIZON*, I rely on different groups of spoons to catch kings off riggers, divers, leads and wires. This is an experiential factor that you need to determine on your home waters. *Every spoon will not produce equally well in all locations within the group dynamic.*

Rigging and running spoons is less involved than flies and dodgers. When targeting kings with spoons most anglers run them *clean*. Running a spoon clean means there is no dodger or attractor in front of the spoon. There are rare exceptions to this, however. If you run a spoon with a dodger or flasher, use a leader of 24 to 36 inches. In the late 70's and early 80's we used metal dodgers and spoons on a daily basis. Today, I believe that flies are far more productive behind dodgers and flashers than spoons.

When running spoons on divers, use a 6-8 foot mono or floro carbon leader of 12 to 20 lb. test. When fishing lead core go with a 14 to 25 lb. test leader. For wire flat lines or suspended ball weights I like a 20 to 25 lb. test leader. For surface spoons running on side planers, go with 12 lb. test in clear water and 14 to 20 lb. test at other times. Use 12 lb. test for spoons run clean off downriggers. Clear blue Stren line works well for light line applications.

Top 10 King Spoons Above 60 Feet

Evil Alewife Silver Streak (sunny/cloudy)
Carmel Dolphin (Sister Sludge) Silver Streak (sunny/cloudy)
Green Puke Stinger (sunny/cloudy)
Piss On Money Grizzly (cloudy)
Purple Stinger (sunny/cloudy)
Green Alewife Silver Streak (sunny)
Magnum Green Dolphin/Glow Back Silver Streak (cloudy)
Yellow Tail Silver Streak (cloudy)
Magnum Kevorkian Silver Streak (sunny)
Ludington Special Stinger (cloudy)

Top 10 King Spoons Below 60 Feet

Blue Dolphin Silver Streak (cloudy)
Green Dolphin Silver Streak (sunny)
Purple Stinger (cloudy/sunny)
Magnum Green Dolphin Silver Streak (sunny)
Old Yeller #5 Diamond King (cloudy/sunny)
Lemon Ice Dreamweaver (sunny)
Blue Oz Mauler (cloudy)
Black/white Yuk (cloudy)
Magnum Green Dolphin/glow back Silver Streak (cloudy)
Magnum Gold Inside/Blue/Green Edge Silver Streak (cloudy)

Spoons and flies catch the majority of my kings. On any given day, baits from one group may produce more hits, so you have to let the fish and the amount of action dictate your selections. Whenever I am targeting large kings, I will have at least one spoon in the water off a downrigger and a lead core. If speed is an issue, or you encounter a strong current, you may want to go heavy on spoons. I find that a mix of clean spoons in a group of dodger and flies is often the most productive spread.

Colors, Colors and More Colors

How many color patterns do you *really* need? Let's be honest, if nothing else, spoon manufacturers have not disappointed us in terms of color choices. Today you can find spoons in just about every imaginable color combination and many of these colors really look good! But guess what, not every great looking color catches kings. Again, how many of these colors do you *really* need? Some people go overboard on selection and too much selection can actually lead to confusion. Too much selection makes organizing and tracking winning patterns difficult.

Target depth is the main factor dictating spoon color. All color patterns do not work equally at all levels. From Mr. Chinook's perspective various patterns will look more or less appealing, depending on the target depth the lure is trolled. When kings are in the top 60 feet the three most productive patterns are the Caramel Dolphin, Green Alewife and the Evil Alewife. The Caramel Dolphin pattern features a burnt red edge and a yellow edge opposite. A glow stripe cuts across the face. The back of the Caramel Dolphin is silver. The Green Alewife has a green edge that fades into pearl with a scalelite shade. The back is silver. The Evil Alewife is basically a Green Alewife with black edging circling the face of the spoon. Other hot patterns for kings in the top 60 feet include Monkey Puke (gold inside, green edges), half green/half gold with a glow stripe, Lime Ice (green edge opposite silver edge with a glow stripe), Piss On Money (dark green body, gold nose, glow with green stripe) Ludington Special and the Mixed Vegetables. Occasionally, gold spoons with a bit of red or rose splashed across the gold will work.

When kings are deeper than 60 feet the two most productive patterns on sunny or bright days are the Green Dolphin, (affectionately known as "Green Flip") and Lemon Ice. On dark, overcast days the Blue Dolphin (Blue Flip) is the number one spoon color. Blue flip features a blue edge opposite a green edge with a glow stripe cutting the face. The back is silver. The Green Dolphin has a green edge opposite yellow edge with a glow stripe. Runner-ups include the Blue Oz, Old Yeller (thin yellow edge on a silver spoon) black face with a pearl back.

Lure companies label their product with a trade name, but there will be subtle color nuances between brands within each pattern. For example, one company may use a darker green, a rosier red or a duller yellow. On the dolphin patterns, some companies have the two colors meet in

Learning the mechanics of lure selection will lead you to great catches of kings.

the middle and other brands will feature a thin strip of silver between the colored edges. Pay attention class! These little nuances are very important and can determine whether one spoon is red hot or not.

Purple, or the Kevorkian pattern, is the one color that seems to transcend all layers of the water spectrum. The Kevorkian pattern will take kings 140 feet down, 20 feet down and everywhere in between. Is this list of colors exhaustive? No, but these patterns are by far my most productive patterns for large kings. Day after day, this group of colors will catch kings.

Some years kings will feed heavily on baby perch. When this happens, lures with a yellow-gold (gold/green, gold/green/yellow and green/yellow) finish are dynamite. In this scenario, you want to use small spoons two inches or less that mimic a perch.

BODY BAITS FOR CHINOOKS

In the early years of Great Lakes fishing, J-Plugs were all the rage . . . then along came flies and dodgers . . . and pretty soon, J-Plugs were past tense. Guess what? During the past several years, J-Plugs have quietly been surging in popularity. Today, many anglers will use J-Plugs and other plugs selectively to help them catch more kings.

Plugs are an excellent choice in three scenarios: spawning fish in shallow water, spring kings on the surface and moody staging kings in deep water. During the fall spawning run, body baits such as J-Plugs, jointed Rebel Fastracs and Rebel minnows, Husky Jerks, Shad Raps and Flatfish, are the leading producers for shallow water kings waiting to head upstream.

In some regions, kings will hang near the surface during the early spring. Under these conditions minnow imitators such as Rebels, Bomber Long A's, Thunder Stiks and Thin Fins will produce off side planers and shallow riggers. During the heat of late summer, staging kings suspending in 100 to 250 feet of water will often become reticent to striking. These large, moody kings will turn up their noses at the standard spreads of spoons and flies/dodgers but put a lone J-Plug or Grizzly in their midst, and you have just uncovered a big king secret weapon!

The most productive plugs for kings are of the minnow imitator and lipless variety. Much has been written on body bait styles and action so the discussion here is minimal. Body baits can be used to target kings off side planers, lead core, wire line, downriggers, flat lines and Dipsy Divers. Speed and lure action are key elements when determining what crank bait to use. Before selecting body baits, determine your trolling speed.

Like spoons, size and color are major issues. J-Plugs in silver, pearl and gold are studs. Jointed minnow and stick bait patterns include black/silver, black/gold, orange/gold, green/silver and orange/silver. Productive plug size will depend on the day so you will need to tweak your selection process to find the daily winners.

Body baits are the least popular lure group among Great Lakes salmon anglers. In terms of numbers of kings caught, fewer are caught on cranks than on spoons or flies. This fact, however, does not disqualify body baits from your tackle box. In fact, there are periods when they will out fish other baits. There will also be days when plugs will put the biggest kings in the boat. In other words, don't leave port without them!

Top 10 Body Baits

Number 4 Silver J-Plug
Number 5 Gold, Red Ladder Back J-Plug
Jointed Black/Silver J2000 Rebel Minnow
Number 4 Pearl J-Plug
Number 4 White Gold J-Plug
Orange Top/Silver Belly Fastrack
Number 5 Green Top/Yellow Belly J-Plug
Jointed Black/Gold J2000 Rebel Minnow
Blue/Silver Rapala Husky Jerk
Pearl M2 Flatfish

Tactics, Techniques and Strategies for Great Lakes Kings

"A lost fish or a broken line is often the first spoke falling off the wheel. Don't let adversity throw you off track—everyone experiences bad luck! Work through the problems and you will overcome adversity and catch trophy kings!"

—Captain Arnie Arredondo

You know, every time you wet a line for kings, you will be confronted with a variety of choices. Believe it or not, how you respond to these choices has tremendous bearing on your success. If you understand all the options available, you will be able to react to the season, weather, and moods of the fish. You will be catching trophy kings all season long!

CHAPTER 8

Light Line Tactics For Trophy Kings

What does it take to catch a trophy? Big hooks and heavy line? A big boat with a heavy rod and reel tied to a big hook? If you want to consistently catch big kings under tough conditions leave the big hooks, heavy line and tuna sticks in the garage. If you want to take your angling to a new level *lighten up!* Spring, summer and fall, a major part of my trophy king program utilizes light line tactics.

Today, with the advent of zebra mussels and clear water, light line off downriggers is more productive than ever. Light line adds a dimension of stealth that cannot be duplicated with any other presentation. Catching big kings on light line is a riot! If you learn to use light line, you will catch more big kings.

Light line fishing is not new to the Great Lakes. My father and I have targeted big kings with light line since the 1970's. Not only did those early fishing adventures bring my father and I closer, they taught me a valuable lesson—you can catch big kings on light line when other anglers, using traditional tactics, were only catching coho, lake trout and rainbows.

Looking back today, from the perspective of a father, I really appreciate my dad's patience! We could have loaded up with heavy tackle and fished for salmon like everyone else . . . but not team *Frick 'N Frack!* The things my dad did for me when I was young! During those formative years we caught huge fish on line as light as 4 and 6 lb. test. Some of those early battles with Great Lakes Goliaths were monumental, but we eventually learned how to take the fight to the fish.

When I went into the charter business I did not forget those early light line lessons. When you fish every day of the week, you have an opportunity to perfect a tactic. By employing light line on my charters, I found that I could catch big kings when my competitors could not.

Now, many people believe you can't catch big kings on light line. Let's be realistic, if you use 12 lb. line and catch a 25 lb. king, you have a 2:1 catch ratio. Catch a 36 lb. king and you have a 3:1 ratio. Now, check out the IGFA line class records for salt water and you will notice loads of line class records for double and triple digit weight fish that are 3:1, 4:1 and much greater. Can it be done? I was on a 31-foot Bertram off the tip of Baja with some clients and one of the guys caught a 140 lb. stripped marlin on 17 lb. Stren line. That's a 7:1 fish! Do the math, 2:1, 3:1 and even 4:1 ratios on Kings are very realistic.

LIGHT LINE TACKLE

Your equipment must perform if you want to subdue large fish on skinny line. This brief discussion on tackle requirements may be redundant for some, but it is critical. For a full discussion on selecting tackle for all Great Lakes applications see Chapters Two and Four of *Great Lakes Salmon And Trout Fishing, The Complete Troller's Guide.*

Let's define "light tackle." For running clean spoons and plugs on downriggers 12 lb. test mono is ideal. When seas are calm and gin clear, 8 lb. and 10 lb. test may add extra fish to your day. When fishing dodgers, flashers and flies off riggers, 17 to 20 lb. test mono is adequate. Seventeen-pound test mono is ideal for fishing mono Dipsies. Most Big Water anglers make the mistake of running mono divers on 25 to 30 lb. test line. The thinner diameter of 17 lb. test creates less drag, minimizing blow back, and allows for greater depth penetration with divers.

You must pay attention when light lining. You need to monitor lines for frays and you need to coach inexperienced anglers when fighting a large fish. I run light line with charter customers. The typical charter customer has never caught a fish larger than a sunfish. The thumb of a charter customer can move with amazing speed and agility to the smoking spool of the reel! Despite the odds, I lose less tackle than most charter boats on my dock, even with my light line and agile thumbed clients. Now, you may understand why a few anglers have left my boat short on fingers!

Rods and Reels

If you are going to tangle with trophy kings on 12 lb. test line, the pre-eminent quality you want in a reel is a super smooth drag. Secondly, you want a reel with a line capacity of at least 250 yards. Beyond these two qualifications, a high-speed pick-up, lightweight frame and a crank that is easy to grip will make fighting large fish more enjoyable. There are a variety of level wind and bait casting reels made by Penn, Shimano, Daiwa, Okuma and Ambassador that fill these criterions. I use Penn

Short rods and skinny line make catching kings a blast!

International 975's for 12 lb. test applications. A word of advice; spend a little extra money and buy top of the line reels. You will save money in the long run through reduced tackle loss and longevity in the reel.

Downrigger rods can be either short or long. Over the years I have used both with great success. Those anglers who favor longer rods of 8 to 11 feet argue that the "buggy whip" action is more forgiving and will result in more boated fish and less broken lines. When my dad and I first started hunting big kings with light line, we used nine-foot rods with great success. We would fish up and down the western shore of Lake Michigan and catch huge kings on our long rods with 6 to 12 lb. test line.

As my angling horizon expanded to saltwater, I learned some new tricks on how to catch big fish. You see I had always been under the impression that you had to use a long rod to catch big fish with light line. I soon observed that coastal and offshore ocean anglers were catching amazingly large fish on short rods. These anglers had perfected the *art* of catching big fish on light equipment. They developed short rods that feature a soft tip but quickly taper into a stout butt. Could we learn from them?

Always looking to improve, I began experimenting with

You will catch more big kings if you learn the art of light line fishing!

shorter rods on Lake Michigan. Eventually, I made the switch to shorter rods in the 6 to 7-foot range. Today, after many line-smoking tests, I believe 6 to 6-foot 6-inch rods with 12 lb. test line are ideal for fishing clean spoons and cranks off downriggers. I use medium light action rods with a soft tip but plenty of backbone in the lower third. You can bend that rod over into a tight arc on the downrigger, but there is enough meat in the backbone to lift big kings.

The attributes of subduing big fish on short rods are numerous. The shorter rods give you more leverage on large fish at the boat. When big kings dive deep, raising them back to the surface with a long, whippy rod doesn't work. The leverage of a short, fast taper rod, allows you to *lift* stubborn kings easily. Again, you are fighting the fish, not the rod. When a big king makes an unexpected turn next to the boat, it is easy to follow the fish with a short rod. Netting fish with a short rod is also easier and the angler and net man can both stay in the boat. When setting lines, short rods are user friendly as it is much easier to set downriggers with a short rod. Short rods are also much easier to store when not in use.

Today, more and more anglers across the Great Lakes are switching to shorter and lighter rods. With proper fighting techniques, you would be amazed at how quickly you can subdue a big king on these short rods! Combine these lightweight rods with small bait casting reels, and you have a rig that is easy to use and won't wear out your arms just holding the rig during a battle.

Now, having preached the virtues of short rods for light lining kings, let me remind you that both short and long rods will work. Of course it is a personal choice and you must be comfortable with your equipment. But, I think once you try short rods and light reels the thrill of the battle will win you over.

Light line spoons and plugs run off downriggers are a stealth tactic. Dodgers, flashers and flies on riggers are not a stealth tactic. Dodgers and flashers should not be run on 12 lb. test line—they will break the line and lead you to the tackle store. When running dodgers and flashers, I recommend 17 lb. test line.

You cannot run a Dipsy on a 12 lb. test rig used with downriggers. For divers you need a larger reel and a heavier rod. Dipsies will be more effective on 17 lb. test mono. Many of you probably think 17 lb. mono is too light for divers. If you reduce your line weight to 17 lb. test, Dipsies will achieve greater depth with less line in the water. This will reduce the stretch factor and result in more hook ups. Seventeen-pound line is also more efficient when fighting large fish. Remember, when you have a Dipsy and a dodger hanging on your line, you have a lot of drag working negatively against you as you fight a fish. The 17 lb. test line reduces the drag and results in more boated fish. When running divers on super line, such as PowerPro or Fireline, go with 20 to 30 lb. test. Look for super line with 8 lb. test diameter.

OK, now that I've convinced you to spool light, what types of rods and reels should you use for divers? For mono, super lines and wire line diver fishing, pick a reel with a smooth drag and a line capacity of at least 350 yards. Remember, if you are fishing divers in a late summer situation where the thermocline is 100 feet down, you may be running the diver out on 300 feet (or more!) of line. Line capacity is critical! A smooth drag is not optional. A line counter on the reel will help you track lure depths.

Diver rods come in a variety of lengths and actions. Pick a rod with enough backbone to support the diver but has a forgiving tip section to offset the smashing strikes that Dipsy Divers seem to draw. Many charter captains favor 8 to10-foot rods for Dipsy Divers. I, however, like seven-foot Shimano and Ocean Master rods for divers.

DOWNRIGGERS, RELEASES AND LIGHT LINE

Fishing is not complicated. People are complicated. We tend to make our lives and the things we do complicated. Fishing line is a perfect example! Historically, anglers have used a section of line to maintain contact between the hook and the angler. Most of the focus was on the two ends of the line: the lure and the rod and reel.

That has all changed in the twenty-first century. While an entire chapter could be devoted to discussing line properties and options, let's focus on three reasons why light line will help you catch more big kings.

First, light line will allow your spoons and plugs to achieve maximum action. Heavy line reduces a spoon's natural action. For example, if you take two identical spoons, place one on 12 lb. test and one on 20 lb. test, the spoon on 12 lb. test will achieve greater fish catching action. This is most notable with lightweight and medium weight spoons. Light line also allows your spoons and plugs to maintain fish catching action at slower speeds of 1.5 to 1.9 Kts. If you run spoons on 20 to 30 lb. test line and slow down to fight a big fish, your spoon rods are dead. Historically, I have caught many big kings when barely moving through the water fighting other fish. These second and third strike kings are typically caught on the spoons set on light line. Without the light line in the water you will miss many doubles and triples.

Once again, I was pondering this thought last summer. In the midst of an outstanding summer king bite I decided to test this theory again. For one week I designated my two corner riggers as test rods. One rigger sported a spoon on 12 lb. test. On the other rigger I ran the identical spoon brand, size and color on 17 lb. test. Every day, the spoon on 12 lb. test smoked the spoon on 17 lb. line by a significant margin.

Secondly, kings are predominantly sight feeders. Today, the Great Lakes are clearer than ever. Many anglers struggle to catch kings during midday when the sky is clear and waters are calm. Light line will open up your midday king bite as it reduces line visibility. This principle also applies to steelhead and brown trout, two other fish with keen eyesight.

Thirdly, light line will improve your hook-to-net ratio . . . really. I believe you boat more big fish after the strike on light line than on heavy line. Have you noticed how the hook pops out of a king's jaw the minute the fish is in the net? How many kings do you think you have lost where the fish didn't quite make it to the net?

Heavier line, with greater line diameter, exerts more drag than 12 lb. test. When a big fish runs out 100 yards of line, additional drag is exerted on the hook in the fish's mouth. When a running king changes direction, heavy line develops a greater belly or loop in the water. This reduces the direct pressure on the hook in the fish's mouth. Lighter line has less drag and allows you to maintain more direct and constant pressure on the hook. Lighter line is also easier to crank in and allows you to "keep up" with a king charging the boat. *With light line and tackle, you fight the fish, not your equipment.*

Before moving on, I must address one very critical component to fishing spoons on light line. Don't take a five-dollar spoon and hang it on a cheap swivel. When light-lining kings, use a small, high quality ball bearing swivel. Big kings and steelhead are notorious for destroying swivels. Use a small swivel such as a Sampo 30 lb. Coastlock. I prefer silver swivels, but I have had success with black swivels. The ball bearing will minimize line twist.

Swivel size is critical! A large swivel will choke the action of most spoons. I can't tell you how many times another captain has walked up to me after a morning's run and asked what I used to catch my big kings. I show him the spoon. After the afternoon charter I will ask him how the spoon did, and he'll usually say, "It wasn't hit." I walk over to his boat, and there is the hot spoon, attached to heavy line with a swivel big enough to choke a coho. A swivel may be a small part of the success equation, but it can shut the entire system down.

Downrigger Releases and Light Line

You cannot have a discussion on light lining kings without addressing downrigger releases. The downrigger release is the contact point where

Use small ball bearing swivels for light line applications.

the fishing line meets the downrigger system. It is the epicenter where a very light fiber mono fishing line is attached to the downrigger weight. Remember, a downrigger release serves two functions. First, it holds the fishing line to the rigger system, allowing you to fish a lure at a predetermined depth, at any depth or speed, without false releases. Second, it must release the fishing line when a fish strikes.

When using light line, how you attach your line to the weight is crucial! You can have the best rods and reels money can buy and the hottest lure on the planet running through the most aggressive school of trophy kings but, if your downrigger release malfunctions then all the other parts of the system are for not! *The efficiency of your entire light line rigger system depends on how you attach your line to the weight.*

A couple of fundamentals to consider when using light line. Eight to twelve pound test mono is thin and light. When using light line you need to protect the line from abrasions that can weaken the line. Downrigger releases are a point of contact. Inappropriate downrigger releases will crimp and weaken your fishing line. If your rigger releases are crimping light line, you will break off fish. The abrasion factor quickly eliminates many releases.

My favorite release is a simple number 12 or number 16 rubber band and a Black's release. They are very easy to use and will not damage light line. Simply moisten the rubber band and loop it around your fishing line two or three times. After each half hitch, pull the band very tight. The band should not slip down the fishing line when pulled against. If the band slips, make an extra hitch around the line. Next, place the band into a Black's release. When the fish strikes, the Black's release opens and the rubber band loop does not break. After boating the fish, simply put the same looped rubber band back into the release. By placing the rubber band into the clip, you can further adjust the release tension by adjusting the clip release.

If you want the fish to break the rubber band on the strike, you have two choices. With the clip release, set the release tension to maximum so the fish will break the band on impact. A second alternative is to forgo the clip release and loop the rubber band over the downrigger weight and allow the band to rest under the lip of the clip attaching the weight to the cable. On every strike, the rubber band will break. The Black's release allows for quicker line resets.

One #12 or #16 rubber band is usually sufficient to hold the line to the weight. If you are fishing below 50 feet, water pressure and current may require two rubber bands to be used. When fishing dodgers or flashers on 17 lb. mono, I frequently use two rubber bands to keep the blade from breaking the rubber bands. If you are getting short strikes, but not hooking up, add a second rubber band (and tighten the Black's release) to get a better hook set. As you gain experience with rubber bands, you will notice a great deal of differences between brands in terms of strength. After the fish strikes, the band should easily reel through the rod guides

A simple rubber band clipped to a Black's release works flawlessly.

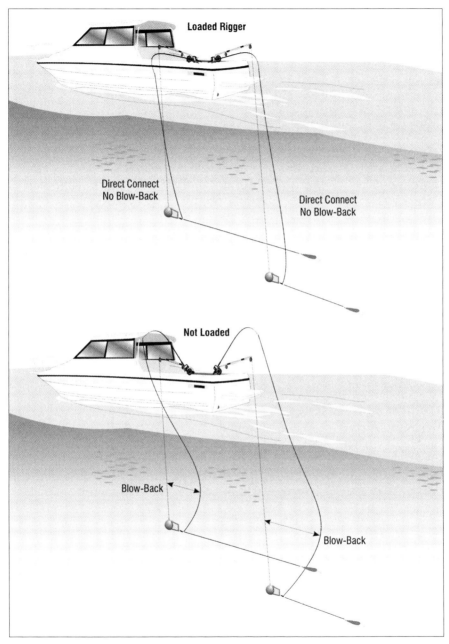

Loading the rigger will result in more hook-ups when fishing light line for deep kings. If you have excessive blowback, fish will have momentary slack line as the line pulls away from the downrigger weight.

and level wind. Number 12 bands will fit through guides easier. Don't leave extra rubber bands sitting in the sun; they will quickly rot.

When setting light line on downriggers you want to *load the rigger* as you drop the weight. Loading a rigger results in minimal blow back (line belly) and is manifested in a rod that is doubled over under maximum pressure. To load a rigger, keep maximum tension on the reel as the weight is going down. When setting a rigger do not keep the line loose or slack as you drop the weight. You want a direct line between the tip of the rod and the release at the weight. How you set light line on riggers is critical to hooking and boating kings after they strike!

Always keep downrigger rods cranked over tight with the tip low to the water and minimal blowback. This will result in better hook-up ratios.

Loading the rigger will minimize slack line when a king strikes a spoon. If your downrigger rod is not loaded, a large belly (blow back) in the line will give momentary slack line to a fish when the line pulls away from the downrigger weight, resulting in a weak hook set. If you have excessive blow back on a rigger, you will have an extra 3 to 10 feet of line off the reel spool (before the fish strikes), depending on target depth. When a fish strikes, you have to pick up the extra 3 to 10 feet of slack before you can firmly hook the fish. If you load the rigger (direct connect), you have no extra line between you and the fish, resulting in a much better hook-up ratio.

Kings often strike a spoon and head straight to the surface. You've been there, the rod bounces hard and pops off the rigger. You race to the rod and start cranking madly only to feel nothing. Fish is gone, no wait . . . he's still there! He's gone. If you have excessive blow back in the line, you will need to crank in the extra 3 to 10 feet of line, before you connect on the fish and put pressure on the hook. A tight line between the rod tip and weight will give you a better chance of keeping up with the king in the opening moments of the fight. The first moments of the fight are critical if you are going to boat a big king. Small mistakes will cost you trophy fish.

A loaded rigger helps you monitor your spoons for shakers, stealth trout (lazy lakers) and light hitting kings, as the tight line will telegraph every tap to the rod tip. If you have a large belly in the line, you may potentially tie up fishing time by unknowingly dragging a small fish around. If you don't load the riggers, you will miss catchable kings on the strike.

This seems like a good place to preach about hook sharpness. When a big king races to the surface, a sharp hook will penetrate their jaw and give you a few extra seconds to hook the fish. Dull hooks will bounce out of their mouth. You will boat more big kings if you use only razor sharp hooks. If you don't like to sharpen hooks, keep a bag of extra hooks handy. If the hook is bent or you miss a few fish in a row, change the hook.

FIGHTING TECHNIQUES ON LIGHT LINE

When talking about light line fishing at seminars, a common question is, "How can you boat a 20 lb., 30 lb. or larger king on 12 lb. test line?" Can it be done? Oh, yes my friends. Not only can you do it, but catching big kings on light gear is a blast! With a little practice, the right rods and reels, and you will be boating kings faster than you thought possible.

You must set your drag so a big fish can pull line off the reel without ripping the rod out of your hand. Most anglers set their drags too tight.

When setting the drag, the fish should be able to pull line off the reel easily, but there should be enough tension so the fish will fight against the rod and work to pull line. Set the drag light on the initial run. Now, 12 lb. Stren is stretchy, so as the fish runs out 50, 75 or 100 yards of line, I like to slightly tighten up the drag. Notice, I said *slightly* adjust the drag. The king can still pull line, but he will work a little harder.

Don't ever put your thumb on the spool and try to stop a king on its first run. Remember, the first run will tire the fish out, reducing the fish's strength, making your job easier. If you don't let the fish run, it will be full of energy next to the boat. A green king next to the boat is much more dangerous than a tired king. If the water is warm at the surface, kings will not fight as hard or as long. If the surface is cold, expect a battle all the way to the boat.

After the first run you need to be patient. You can slowly start to tighten up the drag as you pump the fish back to the boat. When pumping, use steady pumps to draw the fish closer. Drop the rod at a rate so you can reel in line without dropping any slack line to the fish. I watch people fight fish for a living and am amazed at how difficult the "pumping" concept is. Most people pump up too fast and drop the rod tip so fast they give the fish momentary slack line. If the fish is poorly hooked, momentary slack can result in a dropped hook. If the fish is in the middle of a hard run, don't start pumping! If you are pumping and the fish takes off, stop pumping.

Don't be afraid to adjust the drag during the fight. If a fish appears like it wants to make a second strong run, back off on the drag momentarily. You cannot rush a big fish on light line. You need to let the fish dictate the pace of the fight; however, as soon as the fish shows signs of weakening, you need to increase pressure. Once the king is near the boat look to see how the fish is hooked. If the hook looks like it could easily pull, be more cautious in the final moments. If the fish explodes next to the boat, as kings are known to do, back off the drag slightly and let the fish run away from the boat and other lines. Again, it is easier to net a tired fish than one full of energy. When netting a big king on light line, make sure the line does not hit the rim of the net or it will pop.

After catching a king on light line, check the first 3 to 5 feet of line in front of the lure. Kings will often spin in the water and could catch the line on a gill plate or across their back. This could result in an abrasion or nick in the line. That fish may not have broken the line, but the next fish could pop the line at that weak point. Many people become frustrated with light line because they break off fish. The fish they break off are often the result of these small abrasions inflicted on the line from the prior fish. When you are into a hot bite with light line, plan on cutting and retying your spoons and plugs frequently. It only takes a moment, but this will save you plenty of tackle.

If you have never used light line off your riggers, give it a try. Every year I talk to anglers across the Great Lakes region who have made the switch and they all claim to catch more large kings on light line spoons than they caught on heavier tackle. Be patient, and don't become frustrated if you lose some fish in the beginning. You will gain valuable experience with each big fish you catch. Stick with it and I think you will be pleasantly surprised!

LIGHT LINE TACTICS

Light lining kings is one of the most productive tactics for trophy kings all year. When conditions are tough and fish are in a negative mood, light line will frequently out produce all other presentations. Light line tactics have been proven in the heat of tournament fishing as I have won major tournaments with light line tactics under tough conditions. Veteran anglers also know you can blend light line into your regular trolling patterns. The following are some of the light line tactics I use to catch big kings. I usually target large kings with at least one light line spoon rig on all charters.

Bright Sun, Calm Seas and Clear Water

The glorious sunshine is beating down on you and not a breath of wind can be felt within a hundred miles. As you peer over the side of the boat, you wonder if the foot counter on the rigger is working, as the weight is visible 20 feet down. The constant *whining* playing over the marine radio paints a picture of a struggling salmon fleet. Whether you fish on Ontario, Huron, Michigan, Superior or Erie, you will encounter days like this: calm seas, bright sunshine and tough fishing.

If you have spent any amount of time chasing kings, you are well aware that water clarity and light penetration have a huge impact on the feeding patterns of kings. These variables should have an impact on your tactics.

In 20-plus years of chartering, I have witnessed many tranquil summer days when the local charter fleet died a slow death during the midday hours. On those days, my customers were kept busy fighting kings on light line.

This tactic is not complicated. To begin, you attach your spoons to the 12 lb. test line with a 30 lb. ball bearing Sampo Coastlock, or similar ball bearing swivel. You want a small, but strong swivel. Do not put a heavy leader ahead of the spoon. If a spoon has a split ring, remove it, as the weight of the ring will diminish spoon action.

You want the inner group dynamic to be stealthy, so run only clean spoons on your riggers. You can do this with 2 or 4 riggers. If the kings are moody, 2 may produce more hits than 4. Do not put any dodgers or flashers on your riggers, as they will actually repel kings from your lure spread.

When running light on all your riggers, you can put lead cores out on the sides. This will not interfere with your downriggers. Do not run a wire down the middle in this pattern. You can run one diver a side on a 3-setting. The divers will be far enough to the side that they will not shut down your stealth riggers.

When you encounter calm, sunny seas you can also selectively mix several light line rods into your standard group dynamic. Mixing light line into the spread is my favorite way of fishing light line. Often a pair of light lined spoons in a spread of baits will produce most of your big kings on calm sunny days.

On flat calm sunny days run spoons on long leads. Try 50 to 100-foot leads. Now, if your riggers are dead but lead core is getting hit, run the spoons back 100 to 150 feet. I have experienced many days when kings are 30 to 50 feet down in 70 to 120 feet of water and light line spoons on long leads are the only rods producing fish.

If you are running a mixed group of baits try running one light line spoon 10 to 20 feet behind your other downrigger baits. Many times kings will be curious, but they won't fall for the usual baits or patterns. The lone spoon behind the group will appeal to these curious kings.

If you are marking loads of fish but not getting hit, try reducing the overall number of lines in the water. On calm, sunny days kings can become overly particular when it comes to hitting spoons. For this reason, I will change colors more aggressively as I try to isolate a color pattern.

Tracing the Bottom with a Lone Spoon

One of my favorite tactics is to *trace (follow) the bottom with a lone spoon.* A lone downrigger within 1 to 10 feet of the bottom often produces my biggest kings. The spoon and weight are not bouncing the bottom, but are running immediately above the bottom. I prefer to use either of the corner riggers, forming a V pattern in the group dynamic. I will adjust this rigger throughout the day to keep it close to the bottom. If I am changing depths or working a section with an uneven bottom, I will adjust this rigger constantly. At times this lone rigger will be well below the group dynamic.

When following bottom contours, don't set the rigger based on what the foot counter reads. When trolling with downriggers, water resistance creates blowback in the cable. If the counter says you are 65 feet down, factor in drag, trolling speed, weight size, and your weight may actually be running only 55 to 60 feet deep. Remember, the foot counter tells you how many feet of cable are off the spool, not the actual depth at which the weight is running.

When *tracing the bottom,* you should set your rigger from the bottom up! This will give you a more accurate idea of where your bait is running. To do this, you drop your downrigger weight so the ball hits the bottom. Allow the cable to pull back, and drop the weight and make contact with the bottom a second and third time. If you want to run the spoon five feet from the bottom let it hit bottom, and bring it up five feet. As you troll along, every 5 to 10 minutes, go back, drop the weight, reconnect with the bottom, and adjust your spoon's depth. Many large kings strike as I adjust this rigger and make brief contact with the bottom. This seems to pull fish off the bottom.

Downrigger weight size will determine how much cable you need to deploy to reach depth. A 12 lb. weight will have less blowback than an 8 lb. weight. If I am tracing the bottom in over 80 feet of water, a 12 lb. weight is preferred as it gives me more control over lure location. Twelve-pound weights also reduce line tangles when turning or fishing strong current.

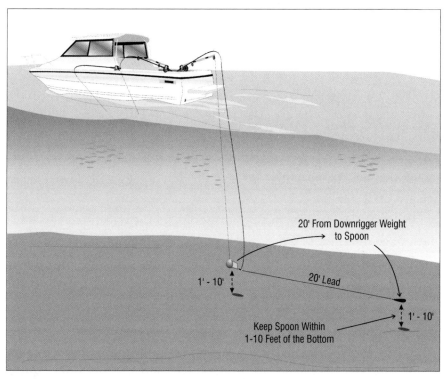

20' From Downrigger Weight to Spoon

1' - 10'

20' Lead

1' - 10'

Keep Spoon Within 1-10 Feet of the Bottom

Light line spoons are deadly for finessing negative kings off the bottom.

Clean spoons on 12 lb. test outperform dodgers and flashers with this method. My favorite spoons for "tracing the bottom" include Silver Streaks, Maulers, Dreamweavers, Yuks and Stingers. Colors vary but some consistent patterns include the Blue Dolphin, Green Dolphin, Lemon Ice, black and pearl and plain hammered silver. Typically, I only run the spoon back 8 to 20 feet when tracing the bottom. If fish are super sluggish, then a 30 to 40-foot lead is employed but the rigger needs to be kept 6 to 10 feet off the bottom.

I have found this tactic extremely deadly for kings that sit either tight to the bottom or suspend just off the bottom. This tactic will produce kings when no one else is catching any kings. While it works wonderfully in the summer, it also works during the spring. If you are not marking any fish by the bottom, don't worry. Kings frequently won't show up on the graph, but this technique will catch kings you didn't know were there!

Spoon and Dodger Tag Team 101

One of the oldest tricks in the book for mixing light line spoons with standard tackle and dodgers is the *Tag Team 101*. Basically, this concept entails fishing your downriggers in pairs. If you have four riggers on your boat, you have two potential teams. If you have two riggers, you have one team. Each team will consist of one light line spoon and one dodger (flasher) and fly on standard tackle.

The Tag Team philosophy is built on the concept of using one dodger to impact two lines. Did you know that if you set a clean spoon on one rigger close to a dodger on an adjacent rigger, the dodger will function as an attractor for the neighboring spoon? Kings will see and hear the dodger, come in to investigate, but may not strike the fly. Many of these fish, however, will hit the clean spoon adjacent to the flasher.

The keys to this system are the horizontal and vertical dimensions between each lure. As you adjust lines, you must always keep these dimensions in mind, as the two downriggers are a team. When kings are the target species I like to run the clean spoon deeper in the water column. Vertically, set the spoon 5 to 15 feet below the dodger rig. Horizontally, set the spoon 5 to 15 feet behind the dodger or flasher. Remember *where* the dodger and fly is located, within your trolling spread, in relation to the spoon. To illustrate, set a fly and dodger 12 feet behind the weight and drop it down 55 feet. Then run a spoon back 20 feet from the weight and set the spoon at 62 feet.

When adjusting bait depths, each individual member of the unit will be moved with respect to the other team member. If you change the depth of one team member, adjust the other rigger accordingly. Keep the *tag team* spatial dimensions within your group dynamic. Remember, the dodger is functioning as an attractor for both lines. You are intentionally working the two lines together to trigger strikes.

There are two ways to run your riggers as pairs. Set up one is to run the two corners as one team. The two booms are a second team. Team one (the two corners) will be set deep. This dodger/spoon team is the best way to target deep kings. The second team is set higher up in the water column. The second team features an open dynamic as the two baits will be fairly far apart, 14 to 20 feet horizontally. The upper team, comprised of an out down on each side of the boat, gives you a very loose or open team. If kings want an open and airy strike box, this method is great. This method is more effective when kings are spooky or holding deep in the water column.

Option two utilizes a boom and corner rigger from each stern corner. This method features two distinct teams, port and starboard. Each team will have a tight horizontal relationship on the perpendicular scale. On this plain, the dodger will only be as far away (horizontally) from the spoon as the two downriggers are mounted on your boat. Now, you can create additional horizontal distance (on a perpendicular plain) if you use a pancake weight on the boom rigger.

On any given day, either option may produce better results. This is an experimentation factor and each day you may have to try both options and let the fish tell you the best method. When you find a vertical/horizontal spread that is working, continue to duplicate those dimensions within your team.

Exact horizontal and vertical variations may vary, so don't be afraid to experiment. I believe dodgers draw many kings into a lure spread out of curiosity. These kings will come in, look at the dodger or flasher and then leave without striking the fly. While the flasher got the fish's attention, it did not trigger a strike. The tag team will capitalize on this situation as the king drifts down in the water column, WHAM! He nails the

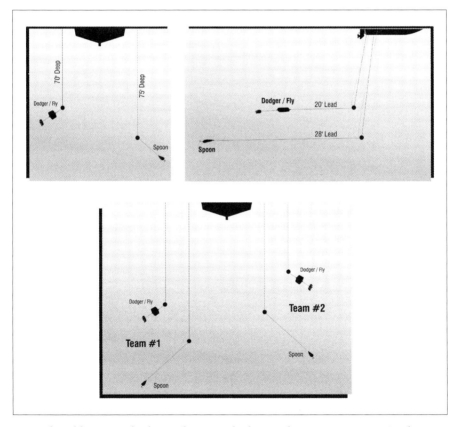

Vertical and horizontal relationships are the key to the Tag Team 101. On the tag team you set the spoon just below and behind the dodger or flasher. The clean spoon often will trigger strikes from kings that were drawn into the lure spread by the dodger. Depending on your boat's beam and number of riggers, you can run one or two teams.

clean spoon. The lone spoon just below and behind the dodger is often too much for fish to pass up!

As you begin to fish your riggers as teams, you will notice certain *teams* of lures will always produce kings. Identify these teams. For example, maybe a white Jensen Dodger and a pearl Howie Fly above a number 5 silver Diamond King always produce kings when you run the team between 90 to 110 feet down. Duplicate productive patterns and line sets. If a Lemon Ice Dreamweaver is on fire 10 feet behind and below a white Hot Spot/aqua fly, keep setting the two lines in the same locations! Salmon fishing is not rocket science; you don't need to reinvent the wheel every time you go fishing.

Negative Kings

It's mid-August and you've anxiously been reading the fishing reports for days. Reports are glowing about the sizzling action and bulging coolers of big kings! You can't focus at work as visions of chrome sided king's flash through your mind. You ponder what lures to use. At night, you awaken to the sound of "zzzzzzing, zzzzzzing," only to find it is till dark

This starboard pair of downriggers is being fished as a team below the surface.

outside and you're in bed. Congratulations! You are fully infected by the bug and the only known cure is a day out on the water battling big kings!

Now, it is your turn. After a full week at work, you are out on the water. Adrenalin pumping, your graph is full of huge marks as you set lines, but you haven't had a strike in over an hour, what do you do? Do you leave the area? Do you frantically change lures until you have tried every lure on the boat? Or, do you lighten up?

If you spend any amount of time fishing for kings, you will encounter this scenario—*negative kings*. Like any fish, kings are moody. Some days, they just seem to sit there and don't want to have anything to do with you. OK, let's be honest, kings are more prone to going into a negative mood than most other salmonids. On Fuzzie's underwater video I was amazed at how many big kings just swam up to his lures, yawned, and drifted away. These are negative fish! How do you catch these fish? After all, my goal is to catch every fish that comes within ten feet of my lures.

Sudden changes (warm or cold) in water temperature (which occur when the lake 'rolls'), or currents can shut kings down. These negative kings are suckers for light lined spoons. I've seen days where hundreds of boats pulling all kinds of tackle pound schools of kings with little action. Now, go through those same fish with clean spoons on 8 to 12 lb. test line, and it's another story.

Spoons such as Silver Streaks, Maulers, Michigan Stingers, Diamond Kings, Grizzlies and Dreamweavers run on 12 lb. test, or lighter, will drive these kings nuts. Some of my biggest kings of the year will be pulled out of these negative schools of kings.

When you encounter dormant kings, don't give up on them. Many times, you will need to be patient. Put on your game face and systematically work the schools. Make trolling passes over and around the fish from a variety of angles. Experiment with your trolling speed as you adjust trolling angles. Some of the very best king fishermen are able to read the currents and make subtle adjustments to angle and speed. These adjustments to angle and current are frequently as important as lure selection.

When you are marking loads of kings, but not getting hit, try adjusting your downriggers as you troll through the marks. When your graph lights up, run to the back and raise one rigger up 5 to 10 feet, and drop another rigger down. Often, by moving the baits suddenly as you go through these negative fish, you will trigger strikes. You will also amaze your friends as you can tell them you *felt* that king and moved the line to intercept it!

As you work these kings, designate key rods as lure changing rods. Don't randomly change lures, rather, change lure combinations. For example, try running one dodger/fly with three clean spoons off your riggers. If that doesn't work, try two dodgers and two clean spoons. Often it is the combination of baits or the way you weave the baits into a complete group dynamic that will elicit strikes from finicky kings. Some days, it's only a matter of isolating a hot color pattern.

Try different lead lengths as you work negative kings. Often, extremely long or short leads will trigger strikes when standard leads fail. Tweak the location of delivery devices within the group dynamic. For example, alter the settings on Dipsies, lead core, wire or copper. Many times Dipsies will attract and excite kings, but it will be the light line rigs that trigger strikes. Even though you may be catching these negative kings on light line spoons, you may still need a few dodgers and flies in your spread to attract kings.

Mid-Day Bite

Many anglers struggle to catch kings between the hours of 9:00 a.m. and 4:00 p.m. This can work to your advantage as many people head home, leaving more room on the lake. All kidding aside, the mid-day bite can be tough for kings. But, you know what? The middle of the day is actually a very good time to catch big kings. On the full moon phase, late morning and early afternoon are the most productive hours for big kings. On clear, moonlit nights, I believe kings will feed at night. These fish are not hungry at dawn, as they have a full stomach. They do become hungry mid-day and often go on big feeds when most recreational anglers have quit fishing.

How can that be? Don't kings feed in the morning and again late in the day? Yes. But, don't large kings need a ton of food to survive? Don't get stuck too deep in the myth that big salmon only feed early and late. Over the years, some of my largest kings are caught at the beginning of the afternoon charter. My afternoon charters typically begin at noon and on many occasions, the biggest kings are caught setting lines, smack in the middle of the day! This is especially true for large kings. The tactics discussed in this chapter can be applied to tough mid-day bites!

Locating a mid-day bite may require you to hunt offshore and locate a deepwater school, or it may be as simple as returning to the location where you caught fish at first light. Often kings will feed hard and shut off at 8 or 9 a.m. Boats pound the fish, and then everyone spreads out. I love to return to these early morning hot spots at about 10 a.m., as the kings will often start hitting again.

Mixing Light Line Rigs with Heavier Tackle

Do you have to run light line exclusively or can you mix a few light line rigs in with standard tackle? Mixing two to four light line rigs into a standard lure spread is highly productive. I recommend making a few light rigs a standard part of every group dynamic you place in the water. If light line is new to you, begin with one or two rigs and start mixing them into your regular lure spreads.

You can run a full spread of Dipsy Divers, wire line or lead cores on side planers with a spread of light line rigs on your downriggers. This past season we had a strong afternoon spoon bite. In the mornings, flies, flashers and dodgers absolutely crushed the kings—but in the afternoons the flies croaked. On afternoon charters I ran four spoons on light line off the riggers and flies and flashers off the Dipsies. Spoons were also run on the lead cores. If you put one dodger down on a rigger, you'd shut down the other 3 spoon lines. Likewise, I believe a dipsy/flasher off each side was helping to pull kings into the four clean spoons. When fish are on the surface, you can also run your side planers without disrupting

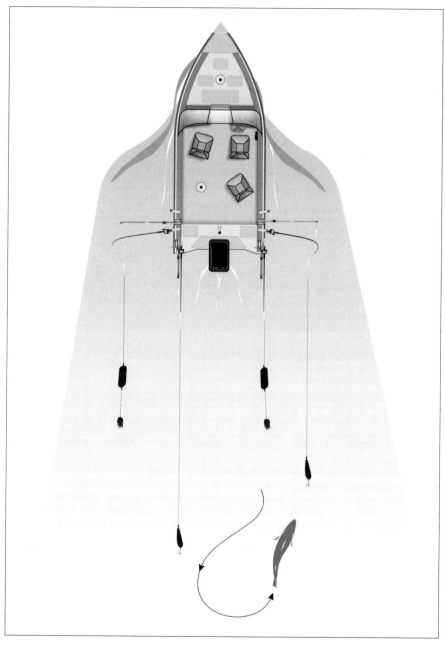

Looking down into the water, you can see how a pair of light line spoons can be mixed in between two dodgers. This basic pattern is very effective for kings; and, it allows you to maximize the strengths of both types of lures.

your light line rigs down below. Light line is very unobtrusive and can be nicely mixed into standard trolling patterns.

Let's illustrate what a mix of light rigs and standard tackle might look like. Run a 12 lb. test rig on one outside or boom downrigger and another 12 lb. test rig on the opposite corner rigger. You would then place one of your standard rods on the two remaining riggers. I will frequently run a dodger or flasher/fly combo on 17 lb. test on two riggers and a light line spoon on the other two riggers.

I recommend running at least one 12 lb. test rig on your downriggers at all times, under all conditions throughout the fishing season. Even if you encounter a heavy dodger/flasher bite, keep at least one clean spoon in the water. It may not always produce as many strikes as the dodger, but it has a long track record of consistently taking the largest king! *The biggest king in the pack frequently strikes the one lure that looks out of place, the oddball effect.*

A Trick We Learned From the Past

In *Great Lakes Salmon and Trout Fishing, The Complete Troller's Guide*, a humorous story gleaned from a summer of charter fishing was used to illustrate how the unconventional can sometimes produce bonus fish. One particular year I had a boom downrigger on my boat that had an accident. The result of the *accident* left that rigger with only 40 feet of cable.

During the spring, 40 feet of cable wasn't an issue. As spring rolled into summer, I just kept setting that old rigger down 40 feet. As the water warmed, and the thermocline continued to retreat deeper and deeper, Dan continued to set that boom rigger down 40 feet. Now, everyone on the dock figured I was reduced to fishing with only three good downriggers. People used to ask me if I was ever going to fix my *broken* rigger.

Well, guess what? Every day I kept setting that old rigger down 40 feet and wouldn't you know it, that 40-foot rigger kept catching fish all summer long! Even when the thermocline was 70-90 feet down, that rigger produced fish. What was going on? Why was a line so high up in the water column catching kings?

From this example, we learned a lot about salmon and trout following a hooked and struggling fish to the surface. This lone rigger, way out of the temperature range of salmon, was drawing strikes when a hooked fish was being fought to the boat. For some reason, fish, especially kings and steelhead, would follow a fighting fish up in the water column and then notice that lone lure not too far below the boat. The amazing thing is, they would strike the lone bait!

By this time in the story, you must be wondering if there was a particular lure on that 40-foot rigger? I tried a variety of lures, both clean and with dodgers, and one lure pretty much earned the right to occupy that 40-foot rigger all summer and fall. Would you like to know the bait—Or, should I save it for the next book? Actually, it was a regular size purple Michigan Stinger. For whatever reason, that one lure was a stud.

What is Captain Dan's point with this story? Sometimes, something out of the ordinary is required to catch kings. How can this story help you catch more fish? When you encounter a strong king bite down deep and the kings are really hot on light lines, but they are spooky and you can only put two downriggers down in the strike zone, consider this out-of-the-box option. Take an additional clean spoon, such as that purple Stinger, and place it on light line and run it on a rigger higher up in the water column. By positioning the spoon high up in the water column, it will not interfere with the deeper lines in your group dynamic. You will not diminish the deep bite by crowding the strike zone, but you will place an additional lure in the water and potentially create a secondary strike zone. This strike zone will have potential every time you hook up with a fish and additional fish follow the struggling fish toward the boat. This tactic does not work every day, but it has put many, many nice kings in the boat!

People often ask me if they can splice a 10 to 50-foot leader of 12 lb. test into their heavy main line and duplicate the success of light line. While this will help your spoons and plugs at the business end, you don't capture the full stealth presentation of running light line through the water. You also don't have the fish fighting properties and sport of a complete light line rig.

CHAPTER 9

Strategies For Offshore Nomads

For years Great Lakes anglers concentrated on king fishing within five miles of the shore. Today, however, anglers realize that some days the best fishing will be found in the middle of nowhere, miles from shore.

Let's face it. The Great Lakes provide some of the most challenging fishing for North American fishermen today. These waters have a wide variety of ecosystems, sub-surface geological variation and subtle water nuances. The shear diversity of the waters we fish and the sharp, seasonal weather fluctuations require anglers to employ a variety of tactics to locate and catch fish. Despite the variety found within the lakes, they do share a common thread: The offshore realm. Believe it or not, from one lake to the next, the basic techniques to locate and catch fish offshore are remarkably similar.

The offshore realm intimidates many an angler. They view this region as a desolate and unforgiving expanse of open water. Nothing could be farther from the truth. Perhaps you need to realign your thinking. Don't approach offshore waters from the perspective of the unknown—that the shear volume of open, unexplored water is too much to handle. Shift your focus and approach the deep blue from your perspective at the helm. Take control!

This fishery is characterized by massive, open expanses of clear blue water that extends to the horizon. The depth over which the fishing occurs can be anywhere from 150 to 400 feet, or deeper. Offshore kings are highly migratory and the nature of the game requires fishermen to become hunters as they prowl vast expanses of water. The rewards for those who persevere and understand the offshore realm are quite handsome, as some of the most consistent king fishing occurs over the deep blue. When the normal near shore and mid range spots are unproductive, it is the offshore honey holes that will frequently save the day.

Captain Arnie Arredondo, who runs the *Phoenix* out of Kenosha, Wisconsin, knows the value of hunting in the offshore realms. During the Bob Uecker Great Lakes Fishing Invitational Tournament, Arnie finished day one with a respectable catch that left him clinging to the top ten. If Arnie was to climb to the top, he needed a strong second day finish. The second day Arnie played a hunch and he took the *Phoenix* offshore and set lines in 330 feet of water, smack in the middle of nowhere! Three of Arnie's first four fish were big kings. Needless to say, Arnie came up with the haul that he needed and the *Phoenix* finished second place for the two-day tournament.

Every trip offshore you will face miles of open water—where do you begin without any landmarks to guide you? Do the same baits and techniques you employ closer to shore work offshore? To begin, offshore king fishing is much like hunting, therefore it is better to think in terms of strategy. Before you head offshore, you need to have a well-designed game plan and methodology in place.

FIVE PRINCIPLES FOR SUCCESS OFFSHORE

Five keys form the framework of successful offshore fishing in the spring, summer and fall. By fine-tuning these critical elements you will react more quickly and adjust your trolling dynamic to local conditions and fish temperament. These principles should guide your search as you prowl the great wide open.

Principle 1. Remember who you are fishing for—*Oncorhynchus Tshawytscha*. This beast likes cold water and lots of fresh alewives to eat.

Use these two key traits, cold water and the need to feed, to help you eliminate unproductive water horizontally and vertically. Horizontally, this will help you set boundaries as to how far afield to wander in search of active fish. Vertically, this will help you isolate the areas of the water column to place your lures.

Deepwater kings really seem to favor ice-cold water. The ideal range of these fish is 42 to 44 degrees. Occasionally, water as warm as 48 degrees or as cold as 39 degrees will hold kings offshore. The need for cold water means you should not even think of fishing until you can reach 42 to 44-degree water. Open water nomads will usually suspend from 40 feet down to 150 feet. Some research being done on Lake Michigan has suggested that kings will go much deeper in the water column. The deepest I have ever caught a king was 240 feet down. Captain Ernie

The offshore realm is home to monster kings.

Lantiegne has caught kings as deep as 270 feet on eastern Lake Ontario. For all practical purposes, however, you can expect to target the 40 to 150-foot layer of the water column offshore. A sub surface temp probe is critical in helping you locate the 42 to 44-degree band of water offshore.

Principle 2. Prepare to go hunting! After determining the horizontal range you will target (8 to 12 miles offshore, for example) be ready to cover some water as you search for active fish. Great offshore king anglers, such as Captain Arnie Arredondo and Captain Dave Engle of Best Chance charters in Saugatuck, MI, are really hunters at heart. When these guys get offshore, it's almost like they have a sixth sense that leads them to concentrations of kings.

Hunting begins the moment you idle down. Before setting lines, formulate a search pattern. Depending on the waves and currents, mentally chart a course—don't just randomly troll around! Should you troll perpendicular to the shore, heading further offshore in search of kings? Or, do you think you found the magic distance from shore and you would be better off to troll parallel to the shoreline? Factor in the conditions that will hold kings: Cold water and bait, and then determine an overall direction of your trolling passes. A plan not only makes you more confident, it also keeps you from trolling back over unproductive water. You will also be more systematic in your approach and will quickly eliminate dead water.

When hunting offshore don't panic if you don't immediately catch kings. On many of my offshore charters, I may spend 30 minutes or two hours looking for fish. Talk about building character, you should try entertaining paying clients as you spend the first hour or two without a strike! Once I find kings, look out, because the numbers start to add up quickly.

Leverage your electronics as you hunt. If you don't mark fish you will want to put on your track shoes and cover some ground. If fish are lighting up the screen but strikes are few, focus on keys three and four and work an area.

Principles 3 and 4. Speed and Direction. These go hand-in-hand. Offshore kings are very speed and direction (angle) sensitive. If the fish are paying attention to speed and direction shouldn't you? I am amazed at the number of charter captains in my region that set lines offshore and then troll to a "destination," usually a pre-determined depth, and then turn around and troll back the opposite direction. No thought is given to angle or speed. This approach is better suited to cutting the grass.

Folks, please pay close attention to your trolling speed and trolling direction (angle). This very well may be the most critical element of the game!

After setting lines, I go into full hunting mode. I don't sit at the radio waiting for a tip. I am the predator, and I systematically begin hunting across the surface of the water, in search of kings. As I troll, I am very focused on angles and speed. Angle is the direction the boat is moving over the bottom, as measured by GPS. GPS is the best way to accurately measure trolling angle. If you measure your trolling path by a magnetic compass bearing, you need to recalibrate your thinking. GPS is far more accurate; as it helps you identify how currents are impacting your troll, lure action and location.

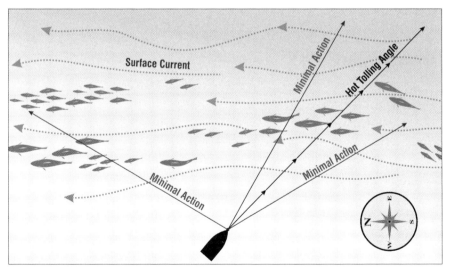

Angle is everything! Slight adjustments in your angle or trolling line, measured as the boat moves over the bottom, can result in increased action. A few degrees of angle can be critical. Top anglers make constant adjustments to trolling angle to achieve maximum results. A GPS and an autopilot will help you fish angles.

If action is slow, I am constantly and systematically adjusting and altering my trolling speed and angle. I may begin by trolling at a 120-degree angle, measured over the bottom. If speed manipulation doesn't draw strikes, I will change my angle by 10 degrees, say from 120 to 110-degrees. Sometimes a more drastic change works—like a 30-degree change.

Remember, every adjustment to the angle may require speed manipulation. As you drop your lures deeper into the water column, you may encounter sub-surface currents. These all have to be factored in.

Don't troll at the same speed for an hour and then change speed. If I am not getting strikes, I will alter my speed every 5 to 10 minutes, looking for the right speed. Every time I alter my trolling angle, I may change my speed. The general range is 1.7 to 2.7 Kts. Sometimes higher speeds up to 3.2 Kts. will work. Experimentation is critical and you need to vary your speeds until you catch fish. When fishing offshore, the speed that works for one direction won't necessarily produce when you change direction.

A GPS is critical to monitor your trolling angles over the bottom and for isolating productive trolling speeds. If you don't own a GPS, you can find some great hand held units for under $200. When using a GPS you want to pay close attention to two numbers: trolling speed and the direction or angle your boat is actually moving over the bottom. When you are trolling for salmon or trout, these two numbers may be the most important numbers of the day. Success is often a matter of aligning your speed and angle. Living between the numbers also allows you to duplicate or repeat successful patterns.

Principle 5. The final key to offshore success is your ability to stay with active fish. When you go to the grocery store looking for a bag of potato chips, which aisle do you search? You don't look in the frozen food section or the fresh produce aisle do you? You go to the snack section. Offshore king fishing is like grocery shopping. You want to spend maximum time trolling over water that holds big kings. What is the Professor trying to say? When you find active, feeding kings in open, offshore water, stay with them. Don't catch half a dozen kings and troll a mile away in empty water.

What are the schooling patterns of offshore kings? Are they tightly packed or widely dispersed? Yes. You can encounter both situations. If you could see beneath the surface, you would find two very different worlds. Some areas are void of life while other regions team with life. These areas with life may be very small in size, covering an area the size of a house or they may be large and cover several acres of water.

Frequently you will find another phenomena: bands of kings that run parallel to the shoreline for miles. Let me illustrate this concept with a common occurrence. When I am fishing offshore I often communicate with Captains from neighboring ports of Waukegan, IL, to the south and Kenosha and Racine, WI, to the north. These four harbors cover a distance

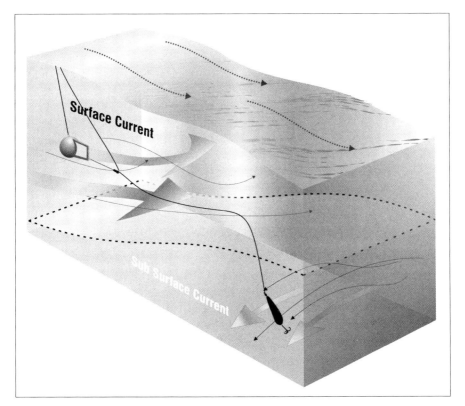

Trolling angle, surface current and sub-surface current are three variables influencing lure presentation at depth. As you troll, you must make adjustments to speed and angle to compensate for these variables—and to trigger offshore kings.

of about 25 miles, yet they share many similarities offshore. On one September day my friend, Jerry Nied, who runs the *Spendthrift* out of Waukegan, was lighting up kings offshore and I was doing the back stroke. You have to understand; offshore water depths vary significantly from one port to another. Rather than ask Jerry how deep he was fishing, I asked him his West Line or Latitude reading. Jerry was fishing two miles outside me! Once I moved an additional two miles offshore, I was into fast king action, yet I was over 10 miles north of Jerry.

Offshore bands of kings may run parallel to the shore for miles. They may be made up of scattered fish or, as is typically the case, many small schools of tightly concentrated kings will be found along the bands. Once you isolate schools or bands of kings, set up trolling patterns to maximize hot trolling speeds and angles.

These five keys should be a part of your offshore king strategy whether you fish on Lake Ontario, Huron, Superior, Erie or Michigan. There is something magical about running offshore and hunting for kings over deep, open water. Offshore king fishing is a battle pitting you, your boat and equipment against nature and the fish. Your only boundaries are the horizon. The rewards are somewhere out there, waiting offshore for you!

TECHNIQUES FOR OFFSHORE NOMADS

Speed Trolling

Every time you head offshore, you face massive amounts of open water. As I previously mentioned, not all water holds fish. The first objective of fishing open water is to locate the fish. Obviously, the faster you troll, the more water you cover. Just to review, I define trolling speed: slow 1.5 to 1.9 Kt.; mid range 1.9 to 2.4 Kt.; fast is anything over 2.4 Kt. No matter what speed range you plan on trolling, you need to run lures that are tolerant of the speed you will be fishing.

If you don't have a clue where the fish are, you may want to try trolling a 60/40 mix of clean spoons and Spin Doctors with Howie Flies. Why Spin

Doctors and not a dodger or other flasher? Spin Doctors are very speed tolerant and they work well at high speeds. This set-up is ideally run with four downriggers, four Dipsy Divers and two lead cores off side planers (one per side). If the kings are in the top 60 feet, you can cover a lot of water using multiple lead cores off side planers at high speeds.

Let's begin with the riggers. Take four downriggers and stagger every other one with a clean spoon. Put a Spin Doctor and Howie Fly on the remaining riggers. Run the clean spoons about 10 to 20 feet further back than the Spin Doctors. I like to set the Spin Doctors back 25 and 35 feet. The spoons are set back 35 and 55 feet. Under calm conditions I may run one spoon off a boom rigger back 70 to 100 feet. You can troll this group

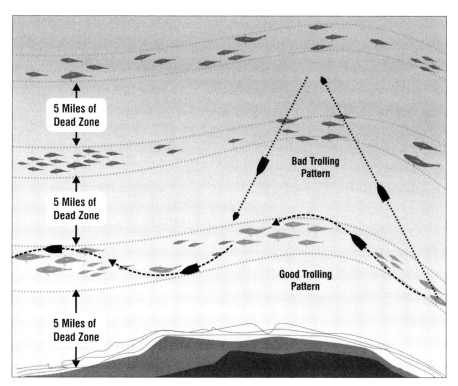

Great Lakes chinooks frequently school in bands running parallel to the shoreline. When this occurs, you will have highways of fish interspersed between dead zones. These bands of kings may run for many miles. This diagram illustrates how to set up trolling patterns to increase your time over fish.

at speeds up to 3.1 Kt. I find it works ideally at 2.2 to 2.7 Kt. When speed trolling, I like fly leaders of 24 to 32 inches.

For the Dipsies I run one wire line Dipsy deepest off each side. I place a Spin Doctor and Howie on these. For offshore kings I always run the flasher or dodger 7 to 9 feet behind the diver. Next, I place one Dipsy off each side on super line. I run the super line Dipsies higher in the water column with clean spoons, such as a small silver Mauler or Michigan Stinger. When prowling at high speeds offshore I like to run clean spoons on all the cores.

This very simple pattern allows you to sift through open waters at higher speeds without sacrificing productivity. Once you locate concentrations of fish, you may want to slow down and start experimenting with other baits and slower trolling speeds. If I cross a section of water and pop kings, I may elect to work the area from multiple angles at slower speeds. If there are kings present, I may change some of the Spin Doctors to dodgers or flashers to accommodate slower trolling speeds.

The Group Dynamic in Open Water

How you craft your group dynamic offshore is paramount to success. Because you are fishing in clear water, stealth techniques are required. Lead core, wire flat lines and copper line are very productive. For downrigger fishing, light line is critical to success. Offshore, spoons are always run on 12 lb. test mono. Dodgers and flashers are run on 17 lb. test line. Many people don't catch fish in deep water because their rigging is too heavy. Kings have good eyesight. Light line minimizes line visibility.

When crafting the group dynamic, I like open and airy lure patterns. In other words, I like to create a lot of horizontal and vertical space between delivery apparatus and lures. I will set the Dipsies on 2½ or 3-settings to put them out to the side. Pancake weights are used on the boom riggers. If you find the kings in a narrow depth range, let's say 65 to 75 feet down; don't put every rod on the boat in that narrow window. Many times, two downriggers will be more productive than four as will be two divers versus four.

When running lead core, copper line or wire flat lines, side planers will add stealth to your presentation and allow you to strain the water. Bottom line, when you are hunting offshore, don't crowd your baits and don't run an exclusive spread of flashers or dodgers.

One Directional Passes

There will be days offshore where you will have massive amounts of action trolling in one direction, and try as you might, you will not be able to match the action when trolling in any other direction. When you encounter this situation, you may want to make long passes on the productive angle. These passes may be 1 mile or 3 miles long. After you make your slide, pick up lines and motor back to your starting point. Set

When fishing over deep water don't be surprised when a trophy lake trout nails a lure intended for kings.

up lines and make another productive slide. When kings school parallel to the shoreline, this method can be quite productive.

Before electing to pull lines and run back to your starting point, really experiment with your trolling angle on the reverse course through fish. At times very slight adjustments to angle and speed may trigger kings to strike.

STAY WITH THE FISH—A NEW WAY OF THINKING

The most difficult aspect of offshore fishing is locating the fish. Don't leave an active school of kings once you find them! One method that will help you stay with fish offshore is to use your GPS and think numerically. There are two approaches to this. You can punch in way points when you have action, and circle the X in the water or you can fish the grid system.

To fish the grid system, think numerically. In your mind's eye lay a numerical grid of interconnected Latitude and Longitude lines over the surface of the water. Rather than fishing between the power plant and the harbor, you are trolling between a north line of 3900 and 4100 in 210

Top 5 Spoons for Offshore Nomads
Ludington Special Michigan Stinger
Carmel Dolphin Silver Streak (regular)
Purple Grizzly
Magnum Purple Silver Streak
Copper/red edge/black spot Michigan Stinger

Top 5 Dodger/Flasher Fly Combos for Offshore Nomads
Blue Bubble Spin Doctor/White Howie
Chartreuse Hot Spot (lead/glow tape)/Tournament Howie
Silver Glow Jensen Dodger/Aqua Glitter Howie
Chartreuse Spin Doctor/Crinkle Green Howie
Blue Bubble Spin Doctor/Double Aqua Howie

to 230 feet of water, for example. This methodology will require you to familiarize yourself with the Lat/Lon numbers of the region you are fishing. As you view the surface of the water, rather than just seeing water and waves, look at the surface as a series of interconnecting boxes. As you troll, you will be crossing off boxes that don't hold fish. When you find fish, you can work the area in a systematic fashion. You can then concentrate your trolling efforts on the *boxes* holding kings.

This numerical or linear thinking allows you to take ownership of an area and familiarize yourself with the region. It will help you identify key bottom structures and will give you a greater understanding of the ecosystem you fish. It also makes a large lake feel much smaller, and this gives you control and ownership over the water!

When you are fishing offshore it is not uncommon to run into schools of steelhead and big lake trout. Kings will mix in with both of these species. Typically, kings will be found below the steelhead and lake trout offshore. If you start catching lakers or steelies, you may want to work the edges of these schools and drop some lines below them.

Many anglers are intimidated by the thought of chasing offshore kings. They view the offshore region as a desolate and unforgiving expanse of water reserved only for steelhead anglers. Nothing could be farther from the truth. Don't let the shear volume of open, unexplored water overwhelm you. If you realign your thinking, you will catch loads of big kings offshore.

CHAPTER 10

Wire Line Techniques And Strategies For Trophy Kings

Step into a first grade classroom for a moment and watch a group of children drawing a picture. If the children have two colors, a green crayon and a red crayon, they will draw a two-color picture. Now, give the children a box of crayons and they will draw a more colorful and complex picture.

Wire line techniques are like a box of crayons. While a full box of crayons increases a child's creative potential, wire greatly expands your presentation horizon and makes you a more versatile angler. Wire offers creative angles to enter the strike zone. It also allows you to insert additional lines into your group dynamic and on the deep side; it extends your reach with divers and ball weights.

While the concept of wire line is not new to Great Lakes fishing, the techniques applied in conjunction with wire line are revolutionary. In the early days of this fishery wire was reserved for dredging the bottom for lake trout. When fishing lakers we would occasionally latch onto a giant king with a wire scraping the bottom. Talk about excitement! At first, the occasional king on wire line was viewed as a bonus fish. But, after enough unexpected bonus kings, a few visionary anglers began targeting kings on the bottom, and suspended, with wire line and ball weights.

As time meandered down the old river, wire line techniques and tackle grew in popularity and productivity. Today, wire line is an integral component of success and is used with a variety of delivery presentations including ball weights, Dipsy Divers, keel sinkers or snap weights, side planers and as flat lines. When kings are way deep and in a negative mood, wire line is one of the best presentation tools available.

Why Wire is a Must-Have Rig on Every Boat

In the world of salmon fishing, wire is the big dollar relief pitcher that wins games in the ninth inning. You should have at least one, if not two, wire line rigs on board. Wire applications are multi-faceted and will produce fish when all other delivery devices and tactics fail. It is a unique presentation option that cannot be duplicated with mono, lead core or super line. Each wire line application is unique and slightly different.

Wire line is a standard application for catching kings on the Great Lakes.

One of the distinguishing factors that sets wire apart from other line applications is the unique action it imparts to your lures. Wire is very stiff when compared to super lines, lead core and mono. It moves through the water differently and reacts to waves and currents in an aggressive, erratic fashion. The result is seen in the way the lure dances through the water. I believe that a wire line Dipsy Diver imparts more action to a fly and dodger than a Dipsy Diver on any other line type.

Wire line has several other characteristics that distinguish it from other lines, most notably, line signature. Every line gives off vibration, or a *signature*, as you troll through the water. The signature of wire is unique and multi-dimensional. Each individual delivery application (Dipsy Divers, ball weights, flat line, side planers) will change the rate and angle of descent of the wire line. The result is that each application gives wire a different frequency or vibration. Therefore, a wire Dipsy

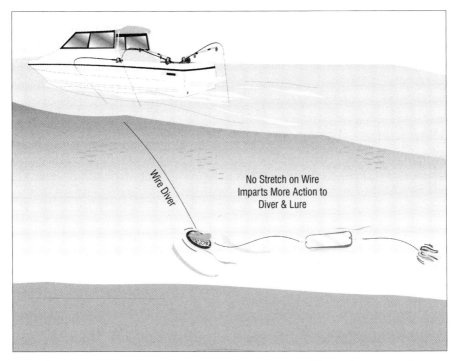

No Stretch on Wire
Imparts More Action to
Diver & Lure

Wire divers impart a unique jigging action to Dipsies and lures that cannot be duplicated with any other application.

Diver has a different signature than a wire ball weight or a wire flat line.

Now, how much does the vibration or frequency attract or repel fish? While theories and sweeping statements abound, no one truly knows the answer. But we do know that king salmon are very efficient predators. They have a highly developed lateral line nervous system that can *feel* vibrations in the water. For this reason, one should not rule out the impact of line signature. I like to run wire Dipsies off the side and have often wondered if just the presence of the wire cutting the water draws fish into my spread. You cannot ignore frequency!

Does wire brand make a difference? Yes. Some wires kink easily, which will result in massive frustration and lost equipment. Today, most Charter Captains use braided wire for kings in 30 lb. test. Some captains will also use 20 lb. test wire. Some of these Captains feel that the diameter of wire will result in a different *pitch*. I recommend the 30 lb. wire, as it is more forgiving and easier to use. Thirty-pound Malin braided wire is the wire of choice. Malin is easy to work with and is popular from western Lake Michigan to eastern Lake Ontario.

WIRE LINE OPTIONS

Wire Divers—The Perfect Match for Deep Kings with an Attitude

Wire line and Dipsy Divers are a potent combination and are true studs for deep kings with an attitude. When kings suspend from 70 to 140 feet down, wire line is the most effective and efficient line application to deliver a Dipsy Diver to the target depth. Wire Dipsies also present your lure into the group dynamic in a way you cannot match with any other application.

Dipsy productivity and performance is significantly influenced by line choice. Line choice determines how deep the diver will travel, how far astern the diver will hang, location of the diver within the group dynamic, lure action and it impacts the signature of a diver. Wire line gives Dipsies their greatest depth penetration plus wire divers have a unique, erratic action and signature distinct from mono or super line divers. Presentation alone can make a difference and there will be days that simply switching your Dipsies from super line to wire will trigger strikes.

To understand why wire and Dipsies are such a productive team lets focus on the signature and presentation of a wire Dipsy. Wire Dipsies impart a unique action (in addition to the lure's own action) to the trailing bait that cannot be duplicated with any other delivery apparatus. Wire is a stiff presentation; there is no line stretch. The wire reacts to every wave and roll of the boat. The net effect on the diver and trailing bait is

huge! Every movement of the rod tip jerks the diver up and drops it back down. Think of what a dodger or flasher must look like as it is *jigged* through the water! I believe this erratic action has more impact on a dodger/ flasher than a clean spoon.

Dipsies also have a unique signature. Believe it or not, fish can *hear* or *sense* the diver with their lateral line. As a Dipsy moves through the water it displaces water, creating turbulence, giving off a *loud signature* or vibrations that salmon pick up on. To understand Dipsy signature, think of the turbulence created by a jet passing through air space. Wire line, in and of itself, also has a unique signature. Because a Dipsy is pulling against the trolling rod, the wire line is

Wire line divers are one of the best applications for targeting way deep kings with an attitude.

stretched tightly. This increases the vibration factor of the line as it moves against the water. Theoretically, many anglers believe a tightly held wire line, being stretched between the diver and the rod, will have a *louder* frequency than a mono or super line. Combine this Dipsy *noise* (turbulence) with the *frequency signature* of wire, and you have a major symphony playing beneath your boat!

I won't spend much time on the basics as the rigging and mechanics of wire line are covered in *Great Lakers Salmon And Trout Fishing, The Complete Troller's Guide*. Basically a large swivel is attached to the wire line with an overhand loop knot. The Dipsy is then attached to the wire via the swivel. You can store the rod at the end of the day with the diver, leader and lure attached (by wrapping the reel) or you can remove the diver, leader and lure at the snap.

While Dipsy Divers come in a variety of sizes and colors, size 1 is ideal with wire. Some anglers use the magnum Dipsy but you need a stout rod to pull this diver and it has a very different action than the size 1 divers. Green and glow are my favorite diver colors for wire. Occasionally the chartreuse diver will also work.

Snubbers and wire Dipsies are a controversial topic. I do not run snubbers with wire divers but some anglers run snubbers on wire Dipsies when targeting kings. If you opt for a snubber, go with the clear stealth snubbers.

I use power rings with the divers for most wire applications. Power rings increase the planning surface of the diver, allowing it to reach greater depths with less line in the water. The rings are particularly helpful when targeting kings deeper than 90 feet or if you want to hold the diver closer (horizontally) to the inner group dynamic. Some anglers opt for the larger after product power rings. These larger rings will result in a sharper angle between the rod and the Dipsy. If you are running two Dipsies off one side, use a ring on the deeper diver. This adds a degree of horizontal separation between the divers and minimizes tangles.

When running a dodger or flasher on a wire diver use a 40 lb. mono or fluorocarbon leader seven to nine feet long. For spoons or plugs go with a 20 to 25 lb. leader. One word of caution: set the divers carefully. If you drop a diver quickly or encounter a strong current, they can easily tangle downriggers, themselves or another Dipsy.

While wire Dipsies can be run directly behind the boat like a wire ball weight, they are most effective when angled to run off the side. When the kings are 60 to 90 feet deep, set the diver on a $1\frac{1}{2}$, 2 or $2\frac{1}{2}$-setting. When kings are below 90 feet use the 1 or $1\frac{1}{2}$-setting. You may want to experiment with the dial setting, as this will determine exactly *where* in your group dynamic the Dipsy will run. A higher setting will plain the diver horizontally out to the side, opening up the group dynamic at depth. A lower setting will hold the diver closer (horizontally) to the inner group dynamic. Positioning of the diver in relation to the other lures will impact whether kings strike dipsies. If the lake is flat calm or kings are moody, you may want to set the diver on a 3-setting. This will move out from the boat a bit and open up the group dynamic. If I use wire divers early in the morning and run them out on 60 to 140 feet of line, I will set them on a 3-setting.

Where do you run wire Dipsies? That's easy, run one off each side of the boat. These two rods can be incorporated into most line set up programs. As you learn the strengths of wire divers, you will discover that many days they will out-fish all other rods. In fact, there are days where you can catch as many kings as you want on two wire Dipsies.

One other reason to use wire divers; when Sea Fleas are thick, wire divers will not collect the little buggers as quickly as super line or mono. If kings are only 40 to 60 feet down but you encounter heavy concentrations of Sea Fleas, wire divers will maximize your fishing time. For this reason alone, wire Dipsies are a must!

How much line do you let out? That ultimately depends on several factors including target depth, trolling speed, currents and sea conditions. In other words, 200 feet of line off the reel will not always put a wire diver at 70 feet. If you are trolling into a stiff chop and your speed is pumped up, the diver will rise up in the water column to 60 feet due to speed and increased water resistance. If you are trolling dead slow on a calm day at

1.7 kts. the diver may actually be 75 feet down. Remember, Dipsy setting and the addition of a power ring will help a diver to reach depth with less line. For example, if you set the diver with a power ring on a 1 setting, it will dive deeper with less line in the water. If you set the Diver without a power ring on a 3-setting, you will need to let out more line to reach the same depth as the diver with a ring on the 1-setting. Actual running depth of wire divers will depend on the texture of the day.

Generally, a wire Dipsy with the power ring set on a 2-setting will dive to 40 to 50 feet with 100 feet of line, 60 to 70 feet with 150 feet of line, 75 to 85 feet with 200 feet of line and 95 to 110 feet with 250 feet of line out and 115 to 130 feet with 300 feet of line. Again, there will be differences depending on the texture of the day. You can increase depth penetration by setting the diver on a 1-setting.

Flies, dodgers and flashers produce more kings off wire divers than spoons or plugs. Remember, wire divers offer a stiff, erratic presentation that jigs flies and dodgers through the water in an irresistible fashion.

The author and his dad with a triple on late summer kings.

Is one dodger or flasher more productive with wire Dipsies? Travel across the Lakes and ask a dozen anglers their opinion and you will receive a variety of answers. While there are many fine attractors available, my three favorite dodgers/flashers for wire Dipsies are the Spin Doctor, Jensen Dodger and the Hot Spot. While colors vary from day to day, the Blue Bubble Spin Doctor, the Smoke Jensen Dodger and the chartreuse Hot Spot with glow tape/lead tape and the white Hot Spot with glow tape/lead tape are consistent patterns on wire Dipsies. Will other colors work? Yes.

Follow the guidelines for fly selection in Section Two. Do other lures work on wire Dipsies? Sure, but on most days you will not find a more productive set up than dodger/flasher and fly.

When you run into kings below 70 feet, wire Dipsies are really the logical choice. Wire is a unique presentation tool that imparts a more aggressive and stiffer action to the diver and bait, allows you to reach target depths, has a nice hum and gives you more control by reducing the amount of line in the water. You cannot duplicate the presentation of a wire diver with downriggers, wire ball sinkers, side planers or lead core. They are unique!

21st Century Tail Gunners

A Tail Gunner in a WW II bomber has a very important job. He must pick off any attacking airplanes sneaking in from behind that were missed by other defenses. A lone suspended wire, a.k.a. the *Tail Gunner* has a similar role in that this lone bait picks off kings that the other baits missed. Running a suspended wire ball weight down the middle is not a secret. In fact, some people have been doing this for ages. What many people don't understand, however, is that a lone suspended wire down the chute is a great weapon to target kings.

The tactic of running a lone wire down the middle is affectionately referred to as the *Tail Gunner* because the suspended wire trails behind the inner group dynamic and places the lure in clean water. Other than lead cores, copper and wire flat lines, the suspended wire (tail gunner) will be the last lure in your group dynamic a king sees. Placement within the group dynamic is important! Many fish are excited by the commotion created by the inner group dynamic, but won't strike. A lead core will be traveling to far astern to capitalize on these curious fish. A tail gunner, which runs closer (horizontally) to the inner group dynamic than lead core, will give these fish one last chance. Frequently some of these curious fish will make the fatal mistake and hit that last bait.

The tactic is simple. Essentially, all you do is attach a 16, 20 or 24-ounce ball sinker to your wire and run the rig suspended off the stern. Once the rig is at depth, you can pass the rod back and forth across the stern of your boat. You can even place the rod at a 90-degree angle out the side. It won't tangle your riggers or Dipsies because the ball weight and lure are trailing far astern of the inner group dynamic.

Target depth, trolling speed, current, sea condition and the amount of horizontal distance you want between the *gunner* and the inner group dynamic will determine weight size. Heavier weights minimize blowback and reduce horizontal spread between the wire and the inner group dynamic. Lighter weights hang further back in the water. Therefore, if kings are holding 30 to 60 feet down, a 16-ounce ball is preferable, as this will create greater horizontal distance within the group dynamic. Some anglers will even use 6 to 10-ounce weights for kings in the top 50 feet.

If you want to reach kings that are 70 feet or deeper, or you encounter a strong current, the 20-ounce weight will give you more control and allow you to reach fish without miles of wire in the water. The 20-ounce weight cuts the water at a sharper angle and reduces the horizontal distance between the tail gunner and the inner group dynamic. When you encounter strong currents or want to reach kings 90 feet or deeper, 20 and 24-ounce weights will allow you to reach target depths efficiently.

Suspended wire rigs deliver lures to the strike zone with a unique action. The stiff presentation of the wire and the erratic action of the ball weight imparts a seductive, hopping action to the trailing dodger and fly. While a dodger/flasher and fly is the most productive bait to run for kings on suspended wires, occasionally magnum spoons will produce kings. In some regions number 4 and 5 J-Plugs are used.

A suspended wire is also a dynamite tool to pry kings off the bottom. Spring, summer and fall, there will be days when kings hold tight to the bottom. Some days the only way you can tempt these fish to strike is with a wire. This tactic is not the same as dragging bottom for lake trout. When you use wire for lakers on the bottom, you drag the bottom hard. The weight and dodger will be making regular contact with the bottom. The result of a properly executed lake trout rub, above the surface, will show a rod that is constantly tapping and jumping. The secret for kings is to tap the bottom occasionally, not pound the bottom. With this approach, the rod will not be dancing, as the weight and lure are not in constant contact with the bottom.

This technique will require you to make frequent adjustments to the amount of line you let out. Remember, you want to keep the lure within several feet of the bottom and occasionally tap the bottom, not plough the bottom. I will occasionally free-spool the wire so the sinker makes contact with the bottom and then reel the line back up a few feet. Once you get a wire adjusted and running at the depth you want it, mark the line with a number 12 rubber band by making several half hitches around the wire. When you reset the rod, this will help you put it back at exactly the same level without all the adjusting.

Can you run more than one wire line tail gunner? Absolutely. There are some charter captains who will run multiple numbers of tail gunners off the back and sides of their boat. Often multiple suspended wires will create too much commotion and only one suspended wire will draw more action. Running a single suspended wire down the middle is easy and will produce big kings.

Wire Flat Line: A New Dimension to Wire Line That Allows Your Wires to Do Double-Duty for Stealth Kings

By now you've heard the latest buzz sweeping the Great Lakes fishing scene, if you don't run lead cores, you're not fishing. Many seasoned veterans such as Dave Engle, Bill Bales and Carl "Fuzz" Styfinski have won major tournaments with spreads of core and no one debates that cores can catch boatloads of fish.

Yet, many Big Water troller's have never used lead core, either because of limited tackle selection (and budget restraints) or they lack additional room onboard to store more rods. Some anglers have used lead core but know the difficulty in running lead or do not enjoy the fight of a fish on lead core.

Did you know wire line offers you an alternative to lead core? A simple wire line rig can nearly duplicate the presentation of lead core. I can also make the wire rig do a few additional tricks that take my lures beyond the range of lead core.

Welcome to the world of the *wire flat* line. Historically, wire has been used with heavy ball sinkers and Dipsy Divers for combing the depths. Wire line can also be used to target fish in the upper layers of the water column. When you deploy a wire line rig as a flat line directly off the stern or on a side planer, you have a unique presentation tool that is similar to lead core.

Wire flat lines are not identical to lead core in presentation as they lack the floating quality of the Dacron sheath. Yet they offer you an element of stealth to target wary fish in *clean* water far astern. An added dimension of versatility is achieved with wire as they can effectively target deeper layers of the water column, beyond the range of single or even

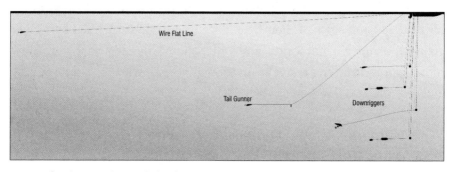

A wire flat line trails much farther astern than a wire Tail Gunner. Both applications are effective, but under different conditions.

double lead cores. While single cores are most effective for fish in the top 50 feet, wire flat lines are effective down to 70 or 80 feet.

When do you reach for a wire flat line? Remember, a common Great Lakes scenario finds kings suspended 30 to 60 feet down and very, very spooky. These fish can be difficult to catch on baits run off downriggers or Dipsy Divers. To catch these fish, you must place your lures in *clean* water, undisturbed by boat noise or commotion, far astern. Wire flat lines run directly off the stern or off side planers will catch these skittish fish.

A handful of keel sinkers from one to 10 ounces and the same wire line rig you use for dropping Dipsies and ball sinkers will get you started. Mechanically speaking, the rig is simple. Take your wire and attach the end to a quality snap swivel. Depending on target depth, attach a one to ten ounce keel or bead chain sinker to the swivel. An eight-foot mono leader trails the sinker. I do not use a snubber with this rig. For running clean spoons use 20 to 25 lb. mono. Dodgers and flashers should be run on 40 lb. leader. You control the target depth of wire flat lines by the amount of weight you add to the wire and the distance off the stern or side planer you run the bait. You can achieve greater depth with less line out with 20-pound wire instead of the standard 30-pound wire. Slow trolling speeds allow the wire to sink deeper.

Lead length behind the boat or planer depends on fish temperament, target depth and boat traffic. If the fish are wary, you will want to run the wire 300 feet or more off the stern. If boat traffic is heavy, you can add more weight and put less wire in the water to reach the target depth.

Let's illustrate with a few examples. If the fish are 30 to 50 feet down, you will only want to use a one or two ounce weight with a 200 to 400 foot drop. If boat traffic is heavy and you can't run a long lead off the stern or a side planer, run the wire back 100 to 150 feet but use a four to six ounce weight. You can tweak your presentation by changing the amount of weight used and adjusting the lead length. More weight requires less wire in the water to achieve depth.

The same lures you use off other delivery apparatus will work on wire flat lines. As you gain experience, you will discover certain lures work better off wire flat lines than others. Clean spoons have less drag and will run deeper than dodgers or flasher rigs.

You can run wire off in-line boards as well as skis. I've only used in-line planers, and usually just on calm days. In-line planers such as the Big Bird and the Church board work well. The Otter release, small Offshore and the Church release all keep boards on the line—just don't crimp the wire!

Typically, I like to run one or two wire flat lines down the chute, setting the rods in the rocket launcher on the sides of the half-tower. These are the same rod holders I use for running Yellow Birds on the surface. If you run two wire flat lines, use different amounts of weight and let the lighter weight out farther to avoid tangles. Most days, one wire down the chute will produce plenty of action.

When setting wire flat lines in less than 100 feet of water, with or

without boards, drop the bait back slowly as a wire with two ounces of weight will sink fast and could grab a few Zebra Mussels. Be extra careful when setting boards over Dipsies.

When kings are 60 to 80 feet down, try running a pair of wire flat lines back 300 to 500 feet with four to eight ounce sinkers. Troll in a slow, curvy pattern and the lures off these rods will rise and sink, driving kings (and giant lakers) crazy and triggering strikes.

A hot lure for large kings is the *old fashioned* chrome number

Wire flat lines can do double-duty in place of lead core.

4 J-Plug off the wire flat line. It works in 50 feet of water and off-

shore over the deeps. This is a big fish rig. Run the J-Plug with two ounces of weight and set it back 200 to 500 feet. When this rod goes off with a big fish, you will find out what a man's arms are made of!

A large part of lead core's effectiveness comes because it runs the bait well behind the boat. When using the wire flat line, you want to mimic this effect, frequently running the wire flat line back 200 to 500 feet. Unlike the lead core, you can target specific depths better by adding more or less weight. When the fish retreat beyond the 50-foot level, just add more weight and send that wire back!

The wire flat line is a great stealth tool that allows you to add extra lures to your trolling spread. Wire has a fast sink rate, and responds very well to adding one to ten ounces of lead ahead of the lure. They can almost mimic lead core presentations and they can give you an added element of stealth for fish in the 50 to 80 foot-range.

Wire Side Planers

Running wire line off in-line side planers or ski's is not for the weak hearted. It is labor intensive and works best on calm seas. It does catch fish . . . but you must be very careful when running it.

The line release is the critical connection. You must not crimp the wire. When using Big Birds, I recommend the small offshore release. I reinforce the pinch-pad with a No. 12 rubber band. To do this, place the wire in the jaws of the pinch pad. Take the rubber band and twist it around the release and wire. Church Boards work fine with their stock releases, but keep an eye on the release's coating, as the wire will eventually wear it away.

Way Deep Kings

Some years you will encounter the dreaded build up of warm water. This unfortunate event typically occurs during the late summer or early autumn when the Great Lakes reach their maximum water temperature. Extended periods of onshore winds can pile up warm water along a shoreline. At times, this will drive the cold water and kings down 80, 90 or 100 feet or more. I have experienced years where we actually had to chase kings 150 feet and deeper! Now, this is not a normal condition, but it does occur. Many people struggle to catch kings but you don't have to struggle.

When the majority of anglers run into this condition, they end up fishing with only two to four downriggers because they don't know how to get additional lines down stairs. Admittedly, when the fish are all super deep, beyond 100 feet, reaching them in a tangle free manner can be difficult.

When you run into super deep kings, you can add three wire line rigs to a full compliment of downriggers with minimal effort. This will call for two wire line Dipsies (one off each side) and a wire ball weight down the middle. For the Dipsies you will want to use the regular or magnum power ring to achieve maximum depth. Set the diver on a 1 or 1½-setting. The wire Dipsy with the ring will have no trouble getting down 100 to 140 feet or more. Depending on target depth, currents, sea conditions and trolling speed, you will need to let the wire divers out 300 to 400 feet to reach maximum levels. The two wire divers will be on the outside of your lure spread. Use caution when turning as long wires can tangle. When chasing way deep kings, white dodgers and flashers followed by white, pearl or pearl/blue flies are preferred.

Run the center wire with a ball weight. I prefer a 20-ounce ball weight on the center wire rather than a Dipsy. The heavy ball weight will require less line to reach deep levels. This will give you more control over the line and result in fewer tangles. Speed control can be tough for way deep kings so make frequent speed adjustments until you connect with fish. Typically, slower trolling speeds of 1.7 to 2.1 Kt. will give you more control when running super deep wires.

A word of caution—when fishing deep wire divers and ball weights let the lines out slowly. You will encounter strange currents and is often best to allow the diver to pull the wire into position. If you are encountering strong currents, reduce the number of lines you are running.

CHAPTER 11

How To Strategically Implement Dipsy Divers For Trophy Kings

The distant rays of the sun had just begun to lighten the eastern sky as I throttled back and the *Blue Horizon* came off plane. After quickly setting the autopilot and letting my clients know what they could expect, I began free spooling two Dipsies into the dark and mysterious depths. Before the first downrigger weight hit the water, the morning silence was shattered by the scream of the port diver rod as a large king smashed the Howie fly. Before the angler could gain an inch on the charging king, the starboard diver rod began protesting as another king tore into the bait and felt the sting of the hook.

Over the next hour, we caught large kings as fast as we could drop the divers. It was rare for a diver to stay in the water for more than a few minutes without getting hit. Welcome to the world of Great Lakes chinook fishing! Many days Dipsies will out produce all other delivery applications.

Despite the incredible effectiveness of Dipsies, many anglers struggle to catch kings on them. Running divers is really an art. If you learn the subtle art of fishing Dipsies, you will catch more and bigger kings wherever you fish. Why Dipsies? Dipsies expand your reach and allow you to place baits into the strike zone in a way you cannot duplicate with any other presentation. Dipsies also produce some of the largest kings each year.

Dipsy Divers are unique and highly versatile presentation tools that accomplish six tasks. First, the diver takes your bait to a specific target depth. Second, they create horizontal distance on a perpendicular plane at depth, by placing your lure to the side of your *inner group dynamic*. Third, Dipsies create horizontal distance at depth by hanging behind the *inner group dynamic*. Fourth, Dipsies impart a unique action (in addition to the lures own action) to the trailing bait that cannot be duplicated with any other delivery apparatus. If you picture a Dipsy moving through the water, it doesn't travel in a straight line. As the diver pulls against the line and fights water resistance, it oscillates and jumps around. Fifth, a Dipsy is a visual stimulant or attractor. Fish can visually see the Diver. Diver color does make a difference. Sixth, and possibly one of the most unique attributes of Dipsies, is the *signature* Dipsies and their lines produce. Believe it or not, fish can *hear* or *sense* the diver with their lateral line. As a Dipsy moves through the water it creates turbulence, which produces noise and vibrations (*signature*) that salmon pick up.

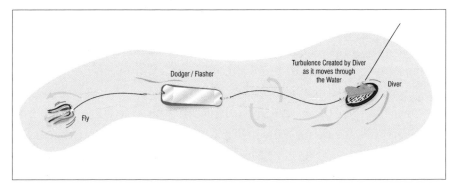

Dipsy Divers are a loud and obnoxious presentation tool. As a Dipsy is trolled through the water, they create a great deal of turbulence and they impart additional action to the trailing lure. This unique signature and action often pull kings into your lure spread.

You cannot duplicate the presentation of a Dipsy Diver with downriggers, wire ball sinkers, side planers or lead core. Dipsies are unique! For a complete discussion on the mechanics of how a Dipsy works you may want to consult Chapter Four in *Great Lakes Salmon And Trout Fishing, The Complete Troller's Guide.*

Many anglers view Dipsies as a means of running additional lines. If that is your attitude, then that is exactly what your diver lines will be— extra, ineffective lines in the water. If you want to maximize the fish catching potential of Dipsies then every time you set a Dipsy line, you need to be aware of these attributes and how they impact the group dynamic. If you learn how to strategically set Dipsies, and leverage these attributes to your advantage, you will catch more kings than you have ever dreamed!

The Six Attributes Of Dipsy Divers

Dipsies take your bait to a precise target depth.

Dipsies expand the group dynamic creating horizontal distance at depth by taking your bait to the side of the inner group dynamic.

Dipsies add horizontal distance at depth by trailing the inner group dynamic.

Dipsies impart additional lure action through their erratic movement.

Dipsies are a visual stimulant. Color matters.

Dipsies have a unique turbulence signature, allowing fish to hear them.

DIPSY SELECTION

While Dipsy Divers come in a variety of sizes and colors, size 1 is the preferred weapon of seasoned king anglers. Green is by far the most productive color for kings. The glow and white divers are very good for way deep kings holding below 80 feet. On calm sunny days when lead core is hot, the clear divers excel for kings suspended 30 to 60 feet down.

The use of rubber snubbers with Dipsies will divide any crowd. I personally do not run snubbers with Dipsies when targeting kings. In the past I have used snubbers, however, I felt I lost more fish at the net because of the snubber.

There are many excellent anglers who do run snubbers on Dipsies when targeting kings. Kings don't daintily nibble on diver baits, they crush them on a dead run! Many anglers believe these bone jarring strikes against the pull of a diver rip the hook out of the fish. The logical conclusion to this thought is that the elasticity of a rubber snubber minimizes the impact on the strike. There is merit to this though. If you set your drag loose enough so a king can pull line on the strike, the diver, I believe, helps set the hook.

If you feel led to use snubbers, go with the smaller, clear stealth snubbers. Wolverine Tackle, (the manufacturer of Silver Streak spoons) makes a small stealth snubber that is an excellent product. The smaller, clear snubbers are a much better choice than the bulkier, colored snubbers.

Dave Mull, editor of Great Lakes Angler Magazine, holds a king caught on one of the hottest rigs on the Great Lakes—a Dipsy Diver, Spin Doctor and Howie Fly.

Power rings add another dimension to Dipsies. Basically, the power ring (either the standard ring that comes with the diver or some of the larger, after market products) increases the planing surface of the diver, allowing you to reach greater depths with less line in the water. A power ring will also help a diver to run further to the side. Power rings increase the surface area of Dipsies resulting in greater oscillation. Increased Dipsy action (oscillation) may be a good thing or a bad thing.

Use of power rings depends on the situation being fished and angler preference. Typically, I do not use the power ring when targeting kings in the top 60 feet. When kings suspend between 60-90 feet, the power ring is frequently used, depending on the currents and moods of the fish. When kings are below 90 feet, power rings are standard. If I am running two Dipsies off the same side, I use a power ring on the deep diver. This adds a degree of horizontal separation between the two divers and minimizes tangles.

A power ring will influence a divers location with the group dynamic. A Dipsy, on 2-setting, out 125 feet without the ring will run at a different location within the group dynamic than the same Dipsy with a power ring. Presentation within the group dynamic (lure location in relation to the other baits and delivery apparatus) is hugely important. Remember, *where WITHIN your group dynamic the Dipsy runs will influence its productivity*. Adding the power ring will change the divers location within the group dynamic.

What about Slide Divers? Slide Divers produce plenty of kings, but they operate on a different platform. Because of all the *noise* and heavy signature associated with Dipsies; they are not a true stealth tool. Slide Divers are a modified stealth presentation. Since you are setting the line behind the slide diver 10 to 100 feet, you minimize or eliminate diver noise. Slide divers escape the direct noise of the boat as they are off to the side 5 to 20 feet, depending on target depth.

When kings want a stealth presentation, Slide Divers are great. Now, be careful when running them, as it is easy for hooked fish to entangle the line trailing the slide diver off the side.

LINE CHOICES: HOW LINE IMPACTS DIPSY PERFORMANCE

The line you run a Dipsy on is an essential part of the Dipsy equation. Line choice determines three key factors: How deep the diver will travel, how far astern the diver will hang and it impacts the signature of a diver.

Before diving into the meat and potatoes of using Dipsies, let me just add a reminder. The lure presentation of a Dipsy is different on all three lines. Wire Dipsies have a unique, erratic action and signature that is very different from mono Dipsies or super line Dipsies. The different lines will also place the divers into your group dynamic in different locations. Presentation alone can make a difference and there will be days where simply switching your Dipsies from super line to wire, or vice versa, will trigger more strikes.

The Impact of Line Choice on Target Depth

The depth you are targeting should be your first consideration when selecting a line to run Dipsies. If the fish are in the top 30 feet, mono Dipsies will work fine. If the kings are 30 to 70 feet down, super line is an excellent choice. Once the fish go below 70 or 80 feet, wire line is the logical choice. Super line Dipsies with power rings can reach depths beyond 80 feet; however, wire line gives you more control and reduces the amount of line in the water to reach target depths.

Of all three lines, mono is the most limited for running Dipsies. Mono features a thick line diameter, yet lacks weight (sink rate). This results in increased drag, resulting in maximum blow back and reduced depth penetration. Mono is a very stretchy line. When you run a mono Dipsy 40 feet deep, you will have to let out close to 200 feet of line. Two hundred feet of mono in the water creates a giant rubber band, resulting in a tremendous amount of stretch. This results in a poor hook up ratio. Mono Dipsies are difficult to use and inefficient once kings descend past 40 feet.

Once the kings are beyond 30 to 40 feet, you should run your Dipsies on super line such as 20 lb. test Fire Line or 30 lb. test Power Pro. When selecting a super line, use lines with 8 lb. test diameter. The narrow diameter of super line will cut the water more efficiently than mono, allowing you to effectively target the 30 to 70 foot-layers. Super line does not have the stretch of mono; therefore your hook up ratio is much higher than mono divers. Super line Dipsies are versatile as they also work excellently for fish in the top 30 feet of water. If you add a power ring, super line divers will work beyond 70 feet.

For applications deeper than 70 feet, wire line is ideal for dropping Dipsies. Wire is heavy and will achieve greater depths than the other lines. Wire also has a distinctive line signature (vibration). Wire is a unique presentation tool that imparts a more aggressive, stiffer action to the diver and trailing attractor and fly. Wire has no stretch and minimal blow back. Because there is minimal blow back, you do not

Dipsy Line Application By Depth	
0-30 feet	Mono
30-70 feet	Super Braid
70-150 feet	Wire

have a looping belly in the line between the diver and the rod tip. Since there is no belly in the line, the boats rolling action is pulling directly against the diver, it is not pulling against the belly in the line. The result: every sway of the rod tip by the boat results in a *jigging* action being imparted to the trailing lure. If you have a blow back belly, the diver is pulling against the line belly, minimizing the jigging action.

When selecting lines for deploying Dipsy Divers, the truth of the matter is that super line and wire line can really be used for kings at shallow, mid and deep levels. If you have a limited budget or rod selection, go with super line Dipsies. These allow you the greatest flexibility and can be used to target kings in all layers of the water column.

If sea fleas, and other line-clinging exotics are heavy, as they can be during August, go with wire divers. Wire's large diameter reduces the build up of fleas on your line. While target depth is the number one criteria for line selection, there are days when presentation will trump depth. Every now and then a wire Dipsy may be the best choice to catch kings that are only 30 feet deep.

Dipsies, Horizontal Relationships and the Group Dynamic

When you're standing on the back deck do you ever look out over the water and wonder *exactly where your Dipsies are traveling in relation to your boat and other lines?* Most people focus on what Dipsies do from a vertical perspective, but they fail to fully comprehend the horizontal dimensions created when using Dipsies. Horizontal distance within the group dynamic is important. Your line choice, along with how you set the diver, has a major impact on where your Dipsy is running, horizontally. Like all fish, kings can be incredibly temperamental. On any given day, the fish may only strike Dipsies that are tightly packed, or they may favor divers that are more aloof and separated from the inner group dynamic.

There are two general horizontal dimensions to consider when run-

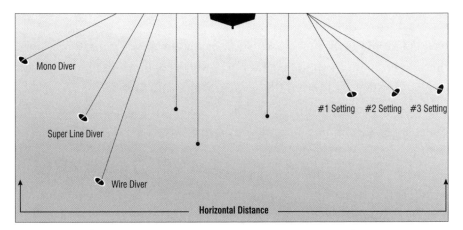

The diver setting and line application will determine how far to the side the diver will run. The right side of the diagram illustrates how a #3 setting will plane the diver further out to the side. A #1 setting will hold the diver closer to the inner group dynamic. The left side illustrates the angle of descent based on line application. If the dial is set equally, wire line will have the sharpest angle, followed by super line and then mono.

ning Dipsies. The first dimension is how far to the side the diver is pulling on a perpendicular angle from the boat and the inner group dynamic. This is greatly influenced by the setting on the diver and line choice. By running the diver on a 1-setting, you will increase the angle of descent, and hold the diver closer to the boat and the inner group dynamic. If you set the diver on a higher setting, 2 or 3, the diver will pull out to the side, creating more horizontal distance on a perpendicular angle away from the boat. A higher setting will also create more instability and oscillation in the divers motion.

There is another element of horizontal spread created by Dipsies. Unless you are running a Dipsy in the top 10 or 20 feet of water, they do not run at a perfect 90-degree angle to the side of the boat. Because of blow back (drag), the divers actually track back horizontally behind the boat as they pull out to the side. This creates horizontal distance between the diver and the inner group dynamic on a different plane. As you increase the amount of line in the water, you will increase this second plane of horizontal separation. Mono Dipsies will display the greatest amount of blow back since mono creates the most drag.

Let's illustrate this concept. Run a mono, super line and wire diver. Set all the divers on a 2-setting, and then let out the appropriate amount of line per application to reach a target depth of 40 feet. If you went under water, you would find the mono Dipsy running further astern. The super line would be forward of the mono diver. And, the wire diver would be closest to the stern of the boat. Rather than putting on a mask and jumping over the side, set a Dipsy to depth, and then pop the diver. Hold the rod and watch *where* on the surface the diver surfaces. Or, as you reel it in, watch the angle of the line as it comes up. Most anglers ignore horizontal blowback.

Is all this important? Yes! Remember, where a lure is running within the group dynamic is hugely important to success. Some anglers will catch tons of kings on Dipsies—right next to people running Dipsies, but not catching any kings. I witness this all the time. The horizontal dimension is one of the secrets to success!

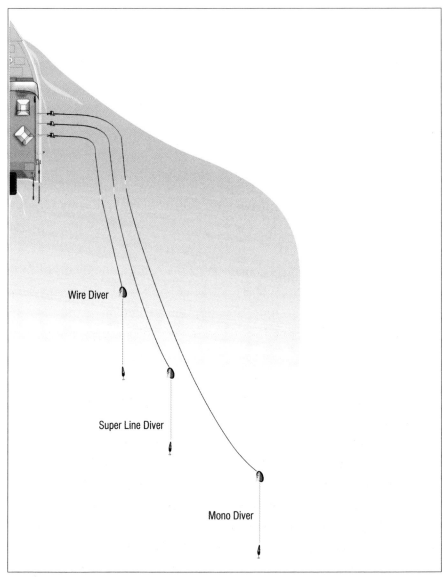

This diagram illustrates how line application and blow back impacts Dipsy location within the group dynamic. If you run a diver on all three applications on a 2-setting, for example, and let out enough line to reach 40 feet, notice where each diver would run. Mono has the greatest blow back and will trail further behind the boat horizontally. Wire has the least blow back and would run closer to the stern of the boat, horizontally, if setting and target depth were equal. Super line falls in the middle.

Line Signature and Kings

I can't quantify how much line signature impacts Dipsy selection. I do feel, however, that we must at the very least acknowledge its potential impact. When using Dipsies, you need to realize that there are two elements influencing line signature: the Dipsy itself and the line. Because a Dipsy is pulling against the trolling rod, the line is stretched tightly. This increases the vibration factor of the line as it moves against the water. Theoretically, many anglers believe a tightly held wire line, being stretched between the diver and the rod, will have a *louder* frequency (vibration) than a mono or super line. Remember, each line type has a unique signature when they are stretched and pulled through the water. From the fish's audible perspective, mono divers sound different than super braid divers, which sound different than wire divers.

Now, you have to remember that a Dipsy will displace water as it moves through the water. It may be that the combination of turbulence, created by the diver, and the *hum* of the line, combine to form a *signature* that is unique. Again, this is theoretical, but many excellent anglers believe there is a fish catching attraction to all the noise and commotion created by Dipsy rigs. There are many days where line choice is critical to the amount of action a Dipsy will have. Signature may be the deciding factor!

Dipsy Tactics

Power Drops for Early Morning Kings

For those of you who start your day early, there is nothing like setting lines as the sun is starting to cast a glow on the horizon. For the uninitiated, this is an awesome time to be out on the water. Kings can be so aggressive at this hour that you will be hard pressed to set more than three or four lines in the water!

To capitalize on this early bite, here is a simple trick to help you set lines faster. Launch your super line or wire line Dipsies first. You can actually set your divers and your riggers at the same time. Take a port Dipsy rod; free spool the diver about 20 feet into the water. Place the pole in the holder, turn the clicker on, and adjust the drag so line will come off the reel at an even pace. You can then drop the starboard Dipsy in and have two Dipsies running out simultaneously and hands free.

The power drop procedure is more efficient if you keep your trolling speed a little hot to help pull line off the reels evenly. Be careful not to drop the Dipsies too fast, as they will tangle. Once the Dipsies are at depth, you can slow down. As the Dipsies are going out, your hands are free to set the downriggers, organize the deck or reel in a fish! Be warned, many kings will strike these divers as they are descending through the water! You will have to tighten the drag when the diver is hit on the way out.

High Dipsies for Out of Temp Kings

Kings don't always follow the rules and a pair of high divers will keep the fish honest. When fishing early in the morning or late in the day, you will

often find that kings will rise up into and just above the thermocline to feed in warmer water. When this occurs, you can add several extra lines to your trolling spread by running a super line diver off each side. You will want to set these lines so they are running higher in the water column than your other lines. These rods will produce many unexpected bonus fish.

To illustrate, let's assume you are fishing in 140 feet of water and the 42-degree water is 80 feet down. The top of the thermocline is 45 feet down. You are

If you learn how to run Dipsies on all line applications, you will catch more kings. having steady action on kings from 65-85 feet down but you notice there are pockets of baitfish marking about 35 to 45 feet down. Run two super line Dipsies out to the side at the 40 to 50-foot level. Set the Dipsy on a $2^1/2$-setting. Kings will rise up out of cold water and feed in warmer water and then retreat back to the cooler depths. The additional Dipsy rods will not interfere with your deeper program and will put bonus kings in the boat.

Lure selection on these high Dipsies will vary. While I am a big fan of dodgers, flashers and flies, don't ignore a clean spoon for out of temperature kings. Kings hanging in warm water may want a clean spoon off a high diver. Two of my favorite spoons for this condition are a small Mauler spoon in silver and a magnum Silver Streak in shades of red, yellow and silver. These two spoons are at opposite ends of the size spectrum, but they both work. My favorite dodger combo for high kings is the chartreuse Jensen Dodger or Opti dodger with chartreuse tape followed by a double aqua Howie Fly or the Tournament Howie (crinkle green with pearl blue).

Searching for Fish with Divers

If you are in search mode, use your Dipsies to help you dial into a hot target level. When searching for a productive level, you will want to stagger your lines across a broad vertical cross section of water. This strategy will dictate using two Dipsies off each side. Each individual diver will be systematically set to target a different depth. You can run all four divers on the same type of line or you can mix wire, super line and mono divers to help locate feeding kings.

One method for fanning a spread of four Dipsies is to set the wire diver deepest, use two super lines to hit the layers immediately above the wire diver and a mono Dipsy could be set to check out the layer above the super lines. Once you locate the level of active kings, you can adjust your Dipsies accordingly. When using Dipsies to help locate kings, you may want to set the divers to run at different depths than your downriggers or lead core lines. Some anglers will run up to three divers a side to help locate kings.

Adding Dipsies to The Group Dynamic

Dipsy Divers are highly compatible with all other delivery devices. During the course of a full charter season it is a very rare day that my Dipsies do not produce fish. Whether I'm in 10 feet or 250 feet of water, they produce fish. While you can scatter your divers randomly almost anywhere in the water column, you should set your Dipsies in a pattern. A systematic approach will help you track Dipsy location within the group dynamic, eliminate dead water and reduce tangles. I like to follow two general patterns. These two patterns will give structure to the group dynamic.

The first pattern is called the *deep drop*. In this model you will drop two divers (one per side) to the outside, deepest corners of your group dynamic. These two divers and one rigger will be the deepest lines in the spread. The overall pattern of the inner group dynamic is M shaped. For deep drops I like to use wire divers or super line divers, depending on

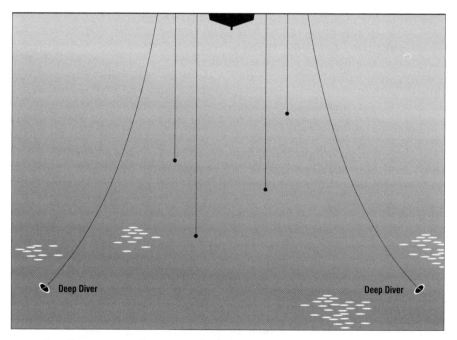

Deep drop divers are used to target the lower-outside corners of the strike box. These are deadly for way deep kings with an attitude!

the target depth. This is my favorite pattern for kings. As the boat passes over kings, some fish will dive down and out to the side. These deep divers, off to the side and slightly astern of the inner group dynamic (downrigger baits) will nail retreating kings.

When you are running a deep drop spread of divers, remember the horizontal perspective discussed earlier! Deep Dipsies really open up your group dynamic. I like to position the deep drop divers (one a side) to run just below and outside the inner group dynamic. Kings will come in and check out an inner dynamic, and drift down and out to the side. These retreating fish often nail deep drops. Diver setting will be from $1\frac{1}{2}$ to $2\frac{1}{2}$, depending on target depth, current and fish temperament. A second pair of divers may be added to the deep drop (one off each side). When targeting kings, I like to keep the second set of divers at least 20 feet (vertically) above the deep divers. Many days the second pair of divers will just get in the way of a hot king bite. Other days they will add bonus fish such as steelhead and coho.

The second strategy calls for setting the divers to run above the inner group dynamic. During late summer, you often find cruiser kings. These

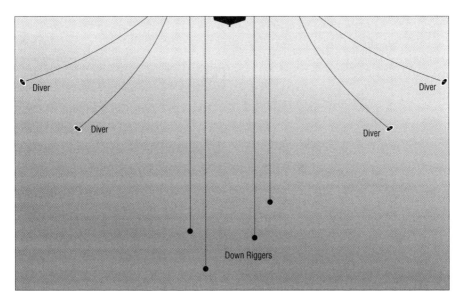

The wing pattern is used to target the upper layers of the strike box with divers.

are fish that appear ready to head up river to spawn. Physiologically, they are more advanced along the road to spawning. They have started to develop the hooked jaw and are turning a beautiful golden brown color. These kings will often cruise up into warmer water layers. They will be above the main school of kings. These fish are often very large.

When I encounter this situation I use the *wing pattern*. Basically, the wing pattern calls for a pair of Dipsies (one per side) flanking your inner group dynamic. These divers are running higher in the water column and out to the side of the inner group dynamic. The overall pattern governing your inner group dynamic is V shaped. These are great tools for sneaking up on big, cruising kings. Set the diver on a 2 to 3-setting depending on how much horizontal separation you want. I like to use super line for wing divers, but mono will work for the top 30 to 40 feet. Both flies and dodgers and clean spoons will take kings on the wing pattern.

Dipsies for Way Deep Kings

True or false: When you encounter way deep kings beyond 100 feet deep, you should put your Dipsy Divers away and concentrate on your down-riggers? The correct answer is a resounding FALSE! When warm water settles in and kings head deep, pull out your wire line and run Dipsies with power rings. During the late summer and early fall, large staging kings will often hug the bottom in 100 to 140 feet of water. Nothing is more productive than a wire Dipsy skimming just above the bottom. When targeting these bottom-oriented kings, you will have to adjust the wire divers perfectly to keep them in the optimum strike zone. If the diver is 10 feet above the kings, they will not rise up and give chase. Therefore, you must dial in precisely the amount of line off the spool to determine the strike level. In other words, don't just dump the wire divers out on 220 feet of line and sit down. Fidget with their depth until you start nailing kings. The effort is well worth it as there will be days when wire Dipsies 100 feet down or more will out fish all other presentations.

This strategy is really simpler than it sounds. It requires one wire Dipsy for each side. Use a power ring and set the diver on a 1 or 1½-setting.

Deep kings seem to favor the green, glow and white Dipsies. When dropping Dipsies deep, let the diver out slowly until you reach the desired depth as Dipsies will spin and tangle if you drop them too fast.

I like to use a dodger or flasher and fly for way deep kings. Spin Doctors, Hot Spots, Pro Chips, Jensen and Opti dodger all work for way deep kings. When kings go deep Howie Flies are the entree of choice. When chasing way deep kings it may be to your advantage not to run a second pair of Dipsies higher in the water column.

This is finesse fishing. Finessing deep, stubborn kings into striking requires concentration. Extra Dipsy lines in the water will divert your attention and may actually cost you fish. Running only two deep divers will allow you to focus on these key lines and adjust them perfectly. One of the best king anglers on western Lake Michigan, Dale Florek who runs the 36-foot Tiara *Noble* will only run one diver a side. He believes that if he focuses on his two divers and his four downriggers, he can dial into kings quickly. I docked behind Dale for many years and I can tell you, the man knows how to catch big kings . . . and he does it with a minimal amount of lines!

Spring, summer or fall, great numbers of kings can be caught on Dipsy Divers.

When dropping divers super deep, pay close attention to currents and trolling angles. The impact of currents can wreak havoc on deep drops, so you may have to adjust your trolling angle to minimize tangles. For example, if you drop the lines deep and notice they are hanging dangerously to one side, alter your course slightly to adjust the lines. Experiment with trolling speed when fishing deep. Speed is super critical. Because of the effect of currents, lures 100 feet down may look very different than a lure running 40 feet down. If the kings are 100 feet down, you need to have your speed set so the lures 100 feet down have the right fish catching action.

When chasing way deep kings with wire divers set the Dipsy release tight. You don't want to pop a diver and have to reel it back in to reset. Also, a tight release will result in more hook ups. When running long wires on the side, watch your turns to minimize tangles.

You can add a wire down the middle, but this may actually make your job above the water more difficult as it increases the opportunity for tangles. When targeting kings in excess of 100 feet down, you will need to put a lot of line in the water to reach the target depth. Depending on trolling speed, current, sea conditions and exact target depth, 200 to 350 feet of line. Also, super deep kings often like a wide-open strike box. Now, you can add a pair of downriggers to the mix without tangles and without spooking deep kings. When running a wire diver super deep off each side, I like to run two corner downriggers downstairs with the wires. At least one of these deep riggers will sport a clean spoon. This four-rod spread is dynamite on way deep kings.

CHAPTER 12

Stealth Kings: Overcoming Clear Water On The Great Lakes

I'll never forget my first sight of a B-1 Stealth Bomber. My wife, Mary, and I were watching our children at a playground in the foothills on the northwest side of Colorado Springs (just south of the US Air Force Academy). For no reason, I looked over my shoulder and there was a cell of stealth bombers coming in fast and low directly over the rooftops! What an awesome, yet eerie sight those planes made! They left everyone speechless. If I had not turned around, I would not have seen nor heard those planes, or been aware of their presence, until they were directly overhead.

Properly executed *stealth techniques* have the same impact on king salmon as those planes had on me. When running stealth tactics, your goal is to present your lures to fish that have not been affected by the presence of your boat or any other unnatural disturbances. You want the presentation to catch those fish so off guard that their only reaction is to strike the bait that just ran across their shoulder.

Great Lakes anglers practice five common stealth techniques: lead core line, light line off riggers, copper line, super line with ball weights and wire flat lines. In this chapter I will discuss lead core, copper line and super line with ball weights. Light line and wire flat line tactics are covered in separate chapters.

LEAD CORE: IN MICHIGAN, THIS IS HOW THEY BUTTER THEIR BREAD

Basic Presentation Features of Lead Core

While lead core is not a new technique, anglers across the Great Lakes have embraced it with great enthusiasm in recent years. Lead core lines produce fish daily, but their real strength is on tough days when kings suspending between 20 to 50 feet down are boat shy. This reason alone makes lead core a key component on any salmon boat.

What makes lead core such a great stealth tactic? Lead core is the ultimate secret weapon because it allows you to run your baits great distances from the boat in *super clean* water that has not been disturbed by boat noise, electronics, delivery apparatuses (Dipsies or downrigger weights and cables) or anything else you can think of. While many anglers have been running lead directly off the stern for ages, enterprising captains now run one, two, three or more cores off each side of the boat. *Lead core off side planers may be the ultimate stealth technique!*

To effectively fish lead core, you need to understand the properties of lead core that distinguish it from other line presentations. Lead core line is a unique combination of lead and Dacron. The center component is a thin filament of lead. The lead is encased in a Dacron sheath. Lead and Dacron exert two very different forces on the line when trolling. The weight of the lead causes the line to sink. The bulky Dacron casing, however, influences the sink rate. While the lead is sinking, the Dacron casing has a buoyant effect on the line, actually working against the lead to *float* the line. The bulky casing also exerts drag on the line, causing the line to actually rise up in the water. This combination of sinking, buoyancy and drag is what gives lead core such a unique presentation.

What does all this mean? The unique properties of lead core give the line a very different presentation. Lead core lines will rise and fall in the water column as you troll and the boat interacts with waves and currents. As the boat turns lead core on the inside of the turn will sink. Cores on the outside will actually rise up several feet in the water. This has a huge impact on lure presentation! Every time you change trolling direction, slow your speed, or increase trolling speed, you change the depth at which your lead core lines are running. When you slow down, cores will sink several feet. When you pick up your trolling speed, cores will actually rise up in the water column several feet.

As you set a lead core line, watch how the line descends in the water.

Needless to say, it looks like the Keating children will catch a few fish in their lifetime! And yes, a little attitude will go a long way.

While lead lines do sink down in the water column, they sort of *float* along, imparting a unique action to the trailing lures. If you alter course and speed a lot, you can impart a unique rising and falling action to your baits.

Lead core will achieve depth, but you must let a great deal of line off the reel to allow the line to sink. It should be noted that lead core does not sink at the same rate as wire or copper line. Wire and copper are heavier and lack the buoyant property of lead core, allowing them to sink at a faster rate than lead core. Wire and copper can reach greater depths with less line in the water.

Just how deep will a lead core reach? Well, this has been debated but in reality, a single lead core, 10 colors in the water, will reach a maximum depth of 45 to 50 feet. A double core, with 20 colors in the water, will reach depths of 65 to 70 feet. A five to seven color lead core will reach depths of 18 to 28 feet. The actual running depth of lead core is heavily dependant on the amount of line deployed, lure selection, line diameter, trolling speed, current and sea conditions. Clean spoons, which have less drag, will reach greater depths than flashers and dodgers. Slower trolling speeds will also result in slightly greater depth penetration. Inside turns will allow lures to sink deeper, then rise up.

When you are on the lake you will frequently hear anglers using the terms *half core, single core* and *double core*. These terms will tell you how much line they have in the water. Lead core comes in 100 and 200-yard spools. You will also hear anglers talking in terms of how many colors they have out. Lead core spools are marked off in 10-yard increments. Every 10 yards is a different color. Therefore, a single core has 10 colors and a double core is 20 colors. Enterprising anglers will also make up custom spools of three color, five color and seven color cores.

Fishing Lead Core

Anglers using lead core for kings have two options. First, you can run cores directly off the stern of the boat. Some anglers will run one or two cores off the stern on every fishing trip. This method is similar to flat lining. The only difference being that lead core will be running deeper in the water column and you will have more line in the water.

To fish a core off the stern, simply put the tip of the rod in the water and slowly free spool the lead line off the reel. A single core off the stern is an easy rod to run. It compliments many other trolling strategies and can be used simply to put bonus kings in the boat. Now, if the single core off the back is getting all the attention from the fish, then it is time to think about putting some cores on side planers.

When you spool up with lead core, you will want to pack at least one hundred yards of backing on the reel. Thirty-pound Power Pro is ideal backing. Attach the super line to the lead core with a Willis knot or a Howie knot. I have also tied a loop knot into the Dacron and used an improved clinch knot to join the backing to the core. When attaching lead core to backing or the mono leader on the business end you must pull the lead out of the Dacron sheaf before tying a knot. There should be no lead in the knot, only Dacron. On the business end, pull out the lead then make a small loop in the Dacron. Tie the mono leader to the loop with an improved clinch knot. For spoons, go with 12 lb. test up to 25 lb. test. For attractors go with 40 lb. test. While you can experiment with the length of your mono leader, I prefer to run only 15 to 30-foot leaders. A shorter leader will impart more jigging action and longer leaders will cause the lure to rise up slightly in the water column.

Lead Core Off Side Planers—The Ultimate Stealth Tactic

Some anglers will skip over this section with a smile on their face because they have experienced the awesome productivity that a full spread of cores off side planers can produce. Others will approach the following paragraphs with fear and trepidation. Yes, running cores off boards can lead you to some of the biggest tangles imaginable. But if you want to expand your stealth game, this very well may be the stealthiest technique to reach kings. Cores off side planers are far more productive than cores down the chute. If you run them far enough out to the side they will not tangle with hooked fish as often as a lead core flat line.

Cores off planers give you a double stealth presentation, and they allow you to do it with multiple numbers of lines. First, you have a three-dimensional horizontal impact on your trolling spread. Since you are running lead core, you will place your lures well behind the boat. You add a second layer of horizontal separation by letting the core out to the side on a side planer. So, following our three-dimensional thinking, when you run a core off a side planer, you add a super stealth component to your lure spread.

The easiest board to use with lead cores is the Church board. The Big Bird also has the muscle to pull lead cores. When attaching the lead core to a planer, attach the backing to the release. If you put your lead core into the release multiple times, it will crimp the lead and lead to break

Greg Magee and Tom Paul show us how lethal lead core can be on kings.

offs. If you want to run less than a full core (10 colors or 100 yards) off a planer, you will want to use a custom spool.

High seas and wear and tear will cause some releases not to work. You can loop a rubber band around the release to hold the jaws of the release tight on the backing. This will prevent false releases. Also, when using the Church board, pin the backing with a rubber band to the black rod on the rear of the board. This prevents the board from sliding down the line after a strike. Simply loop the band around the backing, making sure it does not slip, and then insert the black pin through the rubber band when placing the backing behind the pin.

Many anglers will run multiple numbers of cores off side planers. Some will put up to five cores off a single side of the boat. When running multiple numbers of cores off planers, you must be very careful! First, you must be fishing in an area with minimal boat traffic. You cannot expect everyone to move just because you have miles of line behind and to the side of your boat. Second, make calculated turns and increase your speed while turning.

So, how do you run multiple cores? Greg Magee and Tom Paul on the Blue Fairways introduced me to the awesome productivity of multiple cores off side planers. I traveled to Manistee, Michigan to fish with them and they opened my eyes to the damage cores could inflict on summer kings! We spent a wonderful July morning catching big kings off Big Point Sable. On that morning, no other line applications could keep up with their cores, which popped one king after another!

When running multiple boards you want to maintain a horizontal V pattern moving though the water. Your longest leads will be run off the inside planers closest to the boat. As you move out away from the boat, you will run progressively shorter lines. For example, let's say you want to run three cores per side. Run a full core (10 colors) on the inside board, a 7 color on the middle board and a 5 color on the outside board. You can use your imagination and run just about any combination of cores, just remember, longest on the inside. This is the opposite pattern for running mono surface lines off side planers.

When running multiple planers, be very careful how you set the lines out! As always, put the rod tip in the water and slowly let the lead core come off the reel. After letting it out, attach the super line backing into the side planer release, not the lead core! Then, float the board back, and then apply tension and allow the board to plane out to the side. Since the inside planers are longer leads, their lines will be deeper in the water column. As

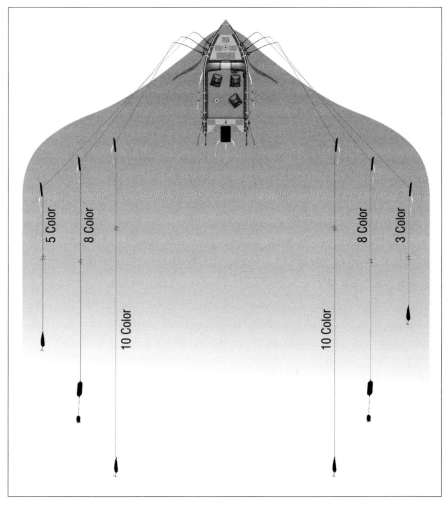

When running multiple lead cores on side planers, run the longer leads on the inside planers. When you view the pattern from above, it will be moving through the water in a V formation with the inside cores forming the tip of the V.

the planer pulls to the side, it will pull the shorter core above the inside (deeper) lines. Sound simple? In reality, it is not that difficult. The real challenge is when you hook a big fish. If the fish makes a wrong turn (from our perspective) you can get some pretty good tangles.

When you do tangle a lead core, rather than toss the line, use the tangled lines to make custom spools of 3, 4, 5, 6, 7 or 8 color cores. Some anglers will splice 5 colors of lead into a full core to make a 15-color lead core line. As I said, use your imagination as you design a lead core trolling spread for your boat. At certain times of the season you will encounter kings suspending in the top 30 feet. These fish can be tough to catch on riggers and Dipsies, but a 5 or 7 color lead core on a side planer is often too much for these big fish to pass up!

Lead Core Equipment

Let's be honest, the reason we run lead core is pure production. If you are looking for a sporting battle, lead core will probably disappoint you. Because so much line is required to deliver full core and double core leads to depth, line capacity is everything. To hold 100 yards of bulky lead core and several hundred yards of backing, you need a beefy reel. If you want to spool up a double core, you'll need more storage space. Many companies such as Penn, Shimano and Okuma make a number of reels that will fit the bill. For running 3-8 color cores smaller level wind reels can be used.

When spooling up, you will want to use super line such as Power Pro for backing. Super line is a superior choice to mono because of the thinner diameter. When mono is used as a backing, it can rot and that will break your heart when the fish of a lifetime makes it into your backing.

Most anglers opt for 18 lb. test or 27 lb. test lead core. Remember, lead core line will simultaneously exhibit two qualities. The weight of the lead in the line will cause the line to sink. The Dacron sheath will create friction with the water and pull the line up. Heavier lead core has greater diameter, creating more drag and minimizing depth penetration. The question becomes, what brand has more lead in their line? To determine this you would have to weigh equal portions of the various brands on a postal scale. Remember, it is the weight of the lead that sinks the line, not the strength of the Dacron. When choosing lead core, you want to consider the weight of the lead and the diameter of the line. Thinner diameter will impact your depth as much as the lead in the line.

Can you attach a keel sinker or snap weight to the business end of lead? Some anglers will run a one to four ounce weight on their mono leader to drop a lead deeper. Just make sure you put the weight on the mono leader and do not crimp the lead core. A weight on the lead core will minimize the buoyant, jigging action that often makes lead so effective. When fish move beyond the range of lead core, a wire flat line with keel sinkers and copper are better applications.

Rods for lead core fishing come from a variety of backgrounds. Anglers on larger boats prefer longer rods for running multiple side planers. This allows them to swing the boards out and steer the line over other lines. Long rods can be difficult to use on smaller boats and many anglers find a seven to eight foot rod ideal. Remember, lead core creates a huge amount of drag going through the water. You want enough backbone in the rod to allow you to pull the lead through the water.

COPPER LINE

You have reels spooled with mono, reels with super line, wire line and lead core. Now, you're about to read a section talking about yet another type of line—copper line. Do you really need to purchase another rod and reel to run yet another type of line? The easy answer is no. This is not one of those presentations that you can't live without, such as wire line or super line. What copper line is, however, is a presentation technique that gives you an additional range of versatility. It is a stealth technique very similar to lead core but it allows you to target greater depths than lead core. The methodology is very similar to the wire flat line.

While copper line is a new technique for most anglers, a few anglers who tend to live light years ahead of the pack, copper line is a standard part of their arsenal. Ernie Lantiegne, the Dean of Great Lakes salmon fishing, is one such angler who has been using copper line techniques on Lake Ontario and smaller inland lakes for ages. Ernie is a big fan of copper. He relies on copper to catch kings when they suspend beyond the range of lead core.

The philosophy, rigging and techniques of fishing copper line are very similar to lead core. The major difference is target depth and presentation. Copper line is much heavier than lead core so the line sinks to greater depths than lead core. Copper line also imparts a unique *jigging* action to your lures when run on side planers, such as Church Boards and Big Birds. When a planer surges with waves, it pulls directly on the copper line, jigging the lure. Since the angle on copper is direct (unlike super line and ball sinkers) you get more lure action. When a side planer pulls on the super line and ball sinker, pulling against the sharp angle of descent between the lure and the side planer mitigates part of the jigging action.

When running copper, 50 lb. test Power Pro is ideal for backing. Just remember, large capacity is needed to hold a spool of copper. When choosing copper wire you want to select a seven-strand copper with a .036 diameter. Diameter is critical, as this is what gives you the 2:1 sink rate beyond lead core. Most anglers who run copper line run it segmented in 300 and 600-foot spools. The actual running depth of copper is closely related to trolling speed, lure selection and sea conditions. An increase or decrease of half a knot will have a big impact on actual running depth. Generally, a 300-foot copper line will run between 50 and 65 feet and a 600-foot copper will run between 90 and 120 feet down. Remember, the slower your speed, the deeper it will sink. Clean spoons will run deeper.

SUPER LINE, BALL SINKERS AND SIDE PLANERS

Is he serious? Does anyone really put all three of these very dissimilar applications on a single rig and then put them in the water, together? Yes, you can place extra rods in the water, in a very stealthy fashion when you combine these three unlikely partners.

The genesis of this technique rose out of the success of lead core. As Great Lakes water cleared up, kings became tougher to catch during the mid day hours. Lead core is effective up to a point and anglers were looking for alternative stealth techniques to catch kings. This method allows you to target wary kings without miles of line in the water and allows you to reach depths of 30 to 70 feet. You also have a horizontal element of stealth with the side planers. This method also places your lures in the strike zone with a unique action that is different than lead core, copper line or wire flat lines. Remember, at times presentation is the key factor triggering strikes.

Thirty to fifty-pound Power Pro is the line of choice. Big Birds and Church boards can handle the drag. Ball weights of 6 to 16-ounces are attached to the Power Pro. You attach the ball weight just like a wire line rig. The lure of choice is a dodger or flasher and Howie Fly. The attractor and fly should be run six to nine feet behind the sinker.

The most challenging aspect of this rigging is setting the line. After attaching the sinker, let the line out 75 to 300 feet (depending on target depth). Attach the line to the board with either an Otter release, Offshore or Church release. Float the planer back (so it clears the riggers and Dipsy Divers) and engage the reel, allowing the planer to pull to the side. You need to be careful not to snag a deep Dipsy line when setting.

This rigging is a new technique that few anglers have tried. Some anglers have had great success with summer kings. The super line sinker rig out to the side allows you to target kings in clean water, undisturbed by boat noise or hardware. It is a deadly tactic on calm days with little wave action. It also imparts a unique action to the fly and dodger as they are just *floating* along beneath the board. Some anglers run multiple numbers of these rigs on a side by staggering the weights. For example, you may want to run a 10-ounce and an 8-ounce rig. Run the heavier weight on the inside planer. If this is new to you, begin with one line per side. It is easier to run on calm days.

If you like to mix and match tactics, you may want to try a tactic that Algoma's Howard Kinn's Captains use with great success. They run a 10-ounce sinker on the inside planer, an 8-ounce sinker on the second planer and then they put a 10 color lead core on the outside planer

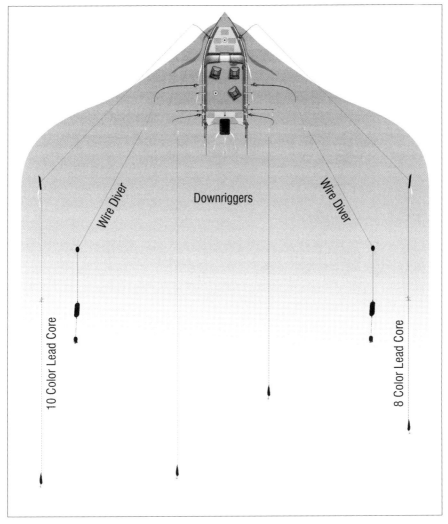

The Blue Horizon super stealth set up is simple, yet deadly. It incorporates two different stealth presentations (lead core and light line riggers) and one standard application, Dipsy Divers. Not only does it produce kings, but also helps you isolate hot patterns and quickly dial into a hot king bite!

board. As you can imagine, if you are creative you can weave a variety of stealth tactics into a dynamite group dynamic!

THE BLUE HORIZON SUPER STEALTH SET UP

If stealth is the order of the day then you may want to try this simple, yet highly effective trolling spread. This spread is particularly effective during mid day hours. It incorporates elements from three different applications: two light line downriggers, two lead cores and two Dipsies. Two of the applications are true stealth presentations.

The two downriggers are rigged with spoons and are run back 50 to 100 plus feet. The divers are run on wire or super braid and set on a 3-setting. A dodger or flasher and Howie are used on the divers. You want them out to the side and away from the boat. One lead core per side is rigged with a clean spoon. You may use 5 to 10 color cores depending on target depth.

Now, the natural temptation with this spread is to put more lines in the water but guess what—more lines in the water may defeat the purpose. This skinny set-up is dynamite for mid day kings! It allows you to present a strong line up of lures in three unique yet stealthy ways.

CHAPTER 13

Small Boat Tactics For Solo Anglers

During the winter months I have the privilege of lecturing at fishing clubs and sport shows across the Great Lakes region. In every crowd one question invariably rises to the surface, "I fish alone from a small boat and am limited to two or three rods. Which rods should I run for kings?" What a great question!

Many anglers who fish solo from smaller boats feel at a disadvantage. If you fish from a smaller boat and feel at odds with the lake, let me introduce two friends, Dr. Art Rupprecht and Jim Flickinger. I have fished with these two men for close to 30 years.

What is special about Doc and Jim? They are two of the most *colorful* and creative fishermen I know. Their philosophy on boat and tackle selection is inspiring as it rivals the ancient TV series, the Beverly Hillbillies. The boats Doc and Jim used were less than 19 feet and were never pretty. Their tackle selection looked like it came from a garage sale. But guess what . . . Jim and Doc could catch fish. They could catch trophy kings by the shore and boatloads of steelhead offshore. Both of these men could keep up with the charter fleet. Doc and Jim are great role models because if you use your mind, you too can catch boatloads of kings from any size boat.

When you are fishing solo, the real key to success is choosing the right rods to deploy. Let's be honest, even when you are fishing with a dozen rods, you will frequently catch the majority of fish on one, two or three lines. If you can learn to pick the right rods for the job, there is no reason you can't catch plenty of kings on your own.

For this discussion I will focus on three rod spreads. The principles for three lines can easily be adapted to four to six line spreads. Most Great Lakes states allow three lines or three lures per angler. Before setting lines, make sure you know state guidelines.

SMALL BOAT ESSENTIALS

Let's begin with the basics; 6-10 rod holders mounted strategically around the back third of your boat will make life easier. (For a complete discussion on small and large boat set up, see Chapter 2 in *Great Lakes Salmon And Trout Fishing, The Complete Troller's Guide*). A minimal selection of fishing equipment would include two number 1 Dipsy Divers, two rigs spooled with super line for running Dipsies, two downriggers and several downrigger rods spooled with 12 lb. test for spoons and 17 to 20 lb. test for dodgers and flies. Your second level of rigging includes one or two wire line rigs, a lead core and additional downriggers.

Dipsy Divers are the best friend of small boat anglers. If you haven't read Chapter 11, go back and familiarize yourself with the subtle nuances of running Dipsies on mono, super and wire line. If you fish alone or from a small boat, Dipsies will make you a better fisherman!

While some anglers catch loads of kings without any electronics, a few gizmos will help you dial into a hot bite faster. The essential electronics include a marine radio and cell phone for safety. A GPS to measure trolling speed and angle (direction) over the bottom is also very helpful. A fish finder will allow you to look for bottom structure and locate bait and predators.

The most useful gizmo for summer fishing on any boat is a sub surface temp probe. You can spend as much as you want, or as little as you want, as a variety of different devices are available. On the expensive end, you can purchase downriggers that measure water temperature at the weight. On the economical side, you can purchase clip-on probes, such as the GMT 40 or Cabelas "Fish Finder Thermometer." Clip the probe to the weight, send it down, and bring it back up to see what the temp at depth is. Both methods work.

The Greatest Challenge Facing Small Boat Anglers

Brad Gregorio is a good friend of mine who used to work for me as a first mate and Captain on the Rainmaker II, III and IV. Today, Brad has entered the real world, but he remains a very accomplished all around angler who fishes regularly from smaller boats. Brad reminds us of the single biggest challenge facing small boat anglers—speed control. This is the number one issue guys and gals with smaller, lighter boats face.

When you fish on the Great Lakes, you will face days with a slight

Small boat anglers can learn much from this unlikely pair, Dr. Art Rupprecht and Jim Flickinger.

chop. These moderately choppy seas are usually the toughest for small boat anglers to fish. If you are in a big, heavy deep V boat, you can cut right through the chop. Smaller, lighter boats do not cut the water with the same intensity and are tossed around by modest waves. Trolling speed fluctuates wildly. One minute you're going 2.1 Kts., the next minute 2.6 Kts. as you surf down a wave.

Are you always at the mercy of choppy conditions? No. Fish to your boat's strengths. Every boat handles differently and individual hull types will *bite* into the waves differently. One hull will fish better at a 45-degree angle to the waves and another boat will do better fishing straight into the chop at a 90-degree angle. Some boats fish great into the waves, but horribly when being pushed by the waves.

Understand this, all waves are not equal and how you identify wave texture and approach waves will have a huge bearing on success. First, identify what angles your boat fishes best. For example, when I fish in steep, closely spaced waves coming from the southeast, I like to troll at a 45-degree angle into the waves. This means, the waves will be hitting my starboard bow at a 45-degree angle. Wave texture varies from day to day and you need to play the angles and troll on angle lines that your boat handles.

The best way to identify productive angles is to use a GPS to measure your trolling direction (angle) over the bottom and your speed. This will give you a true picture of how your boat is moving and GPS speed/angle will help you adjust your speed and isolate productive trolling angles. This very well may be the best piece of advice you will take away from this book. Trolling angle is unpacked in Chapter 9.

Sea anchors are another tool that can help you gain control of your boat and trolling speed. Sea anchors accomplish more than slowing your trolling speed; they actually help stabilize your boat. They also help boats track better and minimize the effects of being pushed around by waves. I believe sea anchors can also attract fish into your spread, but that is material for another book.

A second problem small boat anglers face is trying to run too many rods. Brad reminded me that he will often get into a hot king bite and he will try to put a third downrigger into the strike zone. Often, when the third rigger hits the zone, the other two riggers die. Brad's boat only has a six-foot beam, so when he puts one or two more lines into a narrow strike zone he actually spooks kings and his hot rods quit producing fish. Remember, if you have a limited beam, too many rods in the water column may spook kings. More times than not, less is more.

Choosing the Right Lines to Deploy Throughout the Day

In the morning do you pour yourself a cup of coffee? Or juice? Do you drive to work? Or take public transportation? Or work at home? Do you read a book before bed? Or watch the news? Decisions, decisions, decisions . . . from the minute you wake up in the morning till your head hits the pillow, life is full of choices. Fishing is like life. In fact, success on the Big Water is determined by the decisions you make! It's true . . . the decisions you make will lead to sore arms, or a nice, relaxing boat ride. When you fish alone, you are limited in the amount of lines you can deploy. The key to success is learning when to put out a diver rod, when to rely on light line off your downriggers, or when to put a stealth rig in the water. There are a few basic line tactics that you can rely on.

Regardless of boat size or the number of lines in the water, how you reach the strike zone is hugely important. On any given day, kings will respond better to lures off downriggers versus Dipsy Divers, and vice versa. On another day kings will strike lead core but ignore wire line. For this reason, every day is a new day and you will have to determine the best combination of lines. The solo angler needs to intentionally and systematically select and use two or three lines to dial into fish.

Many solo anglers feel they are at a disadvantage because they cannot run as many lines and lures as their friends on larger boats. Guess what, sometimes that is an advantage. In today's world of ever-expanding choices, many anglers can actually hurt their production by getting too many lines in the water. These anglers actually confuse their presentation (and themselves!) because they want to try all the new lures, flashers and colors. The more stuff they put in the water, the more difficult it becomes to keep track of their group dynamic, and the reality of it is, that at times, the group dynamic and systematic lure selection can get away from you.

When you are fishing from a small boat you have a huge stealth advantage. Since you are legally limited in rod selection, you will have minimal clutter and noise in your trolling spread. Since you are only running three lines (six if you bring a friend) you will be very focused on those lines. This is an advantage, as you will always know where those lines are in relation to one another. When you have fewer rods in the water, you also tend to fish the lines much harder. You will be more intentional with placement and you will track your lure selection. When you locate a school of big kings, small boats have a smaller turning

Kings are an ideal target for small boat anglers.

radius, allowing you to thoroughly work the school. I know many small boat anglers who catch just as many fish as the big charter boats and they do it with a minimal selection of accessories. Fish to your strengths.

To help you understand how to build a solo line spread, I have illustrated several line options based on very specific scenarios you could encounter on any of the Great Lakes. As you gain experience, you will want to tweak these basic line paradigms and build your own models.

Early Morning Attack

If you are an early riser, early morning is a great time to be out on the water. Kings are highly aggressive and often come in closer to the shore during the pre-dawn hours. If you are setting lines at or before sunrise, begin with two Dipsy Divers (one on each side) and one downrigger. Dipsies are one of the hottest set ups for early morning kings. Super line is a good choice for early action as it allows you to target multiple layers of the water column without having to change rods.

Your third rod will be a downrigger. The rigger will be the deepest line in your spread running below the divers. Depending on the depth of the thermocline and the 42-degree water, you may be targeting the 30 to 40-foot layer or anywhere from 40 to 100 feet down. Use basic king finding tactics discussed in Section 1 of this book. If you are on the water and can still see stars, early morning kings often rise higher in the water column to feed. Dipsies are great tools for hitting these fish.

Let's illustrate with an example. Let's say you are fishing in 70 feet of water and cold water (42 to 44 degrees) is on the bottom. The top of the thermocline is at 40 feet. Set one Dipsy to run 40 to 45 feet down (120 to 140 feet on wire, 160 feet on super line) and set the other Dipsy to run about 50 to 55 feet down (160 feet of wire, 180 feet on super line). Next, run your lone downrigger down 60 to 70 feet. As the sun comes up, or you dial into a hot pattern, you will want to adjust your lines accordingly.

If early morning king action slows, you may want to drop your rigs deeper into the water column. If the kings have *disappeared* you will have to ask the question, "Are they sitting on the bottom directly below where you caught them earlier or did they slide out to deeper water?" If you slide out deeper you will have to determine if the kings moved offshore horizontally (suspending at the same level they were holding earlier in the morning) or did they sink deeper in the water column? When trying to determine the new strike zone you will need to make decisions about readjusting your lines. If one line is getting hit, leave it alone! Use the non-productive rods to search new levels.

When making decisions, listen to the fish. Fishermen today make the mistake of ignoring their immediate surroundings. This approach is one-dimensional and neglects a very important source of data . . . the fish and the water they are swimming in. Let the fish, or the lack of fish help you make decisions! If you have three lines in the water, two super line divers and a rigger, and the lone downrigger is catching all the fish, what should you do? Option one is to pull one of your Dipsies and add a second downrigger. If the rigger is substantially deeper than the two divers, you have two choices. You can drop a Dipsy deeper or you can change from a super line Dipsy to a wire line Dipsy.

Afternoon Fishing for the Lone Angler

Do you like to end your day by escaping out onto the water? If you start fishing between 2:00 p.m. and 4:00 p.m. begin with two downriggers and one Dipsy Diver. Set the riggers deep to cover the cold water layers and run the Dipsy above the riggers on either super line or wire line. The depth you are targeting will determine the line application for the divers. If the fish are deeper than 70 feet use a wire diver. If the kings are in the top 70 feet, a super line diver will do the job.

If the fish are suspending in the 30 to 60 foot level you may elect to run two lead cores off side planers and one super line Dipsy. Try a 10 color and an 8 color core to begin. I have experienced many days on my charter boat where two lead cores and two divers catch 80 percent of my kings.

As the afternoon turns into evening, kings will often rise up in the water column and move shoreward. If you are on the water for this amazing time of day you will want to move your lines up in the water column as the kings feed. At times you can just raise your downriggers in the water column. Now, if your lone Dipsy rod is taking all the hits, pull one of your downriggers and add a second diver rod. Also, as dusk approaches, you will want to revert to an early morning line set up.

Spring Kings Solo

When targeting kings during the spring months, you have a variety of options. Since I catch the majority of spring kings on downriggers, I would begin with two riggers and one Dipsy Diver. Spring kings relate to bottom structure and riggers run in the bottom layers of the water column are great for prying big kings off structure. Run one rigger within 5 to 10 feet of the bottom and set the second rigger somewhere in the lower half of the water column. Move the second rigger around and try to locate a productive level. Never set the higher rigger within 10 feet of the deep rigger. Next, run a Dipsy to cover higher layers in the water column.

In some locations, lead core is the favored presentation method for spring kings. If this is the case, two lead cores and one downrigger would be your opening three-line spread. Some very good lead core anglers like to run a full core and a half core for spring kings.

On Lakes Ontario and Huron, spring kings are frequently caught on the surface. If this is your destination, you would want to run your three lines on the surface. Three side planers with body baits or clean spoons would be your beginning spread. If action is slow, pull one of the planers and add a Dipsy Diver to see if the kings are holding deep.

Fall Kings on the Beach

In all the years I've been chartering, some of my most humbling experiences occurs each fall off river and harbor mouths. It is here, when kings are making the mad dash home, that I have had my butt kicked by small boats. Some days I spend about 30 to 40 percent of my time *fishing*. The balance of my time was spent frantically jockeying for position as my customers kept asking why the guy in the 16-foot Lund is netting another giant fish? Then the wise guy in the corner asks why we are not trolling where the fish are! The guys in the small boats had a huge advantage because they were on top of the fish one hundred percent of the time!

Small boats by nature are highly maneuverable and stealthy, which is ideal off pier heads and river mouths. I used to *paddle troll* a canoe for kings. Small boats running three to six lines can turn on a dime. Maneuverability and stealth are frequently more important during the fall than all the firepower and good looks in the world.

So, you have a day to yourself and you hear the kings are swarming the pier heads, what three lines do you run? This depends first on where you are fishing, how deep of water you are fishing and boat traffic. If boat traffic is heavy, you will not be able to run side planers so go with one flat

Learning to choose which rods to run is paramount to success.

line, one downrigger and one Dipsy Diver. If you're off pier heads in 20 to 30 feet of water, and the kings are holding toward the bottom you may want to run two riggers and one Dipsy. If you are working the beach (6 to 12 feet of water) off a creek mouth, two side planers (one per side) and a flat line is perfect. Never under-estimate the power of a lone flat line down the middle for fall kings. I love to run a flat line (20 lb. Fire Line with a six foot mono leader) with a number 5-J Plug 70 to 150 feet back.

When my dad and I used to fish together, we would run two riggers and two flat lines. If we wanted to make a hard turn, we'd shorten the flat lines and spin around. We were very efficient and spent most of our time on top of fish. If I am running a full compliment of lines on my larger charter boat, I do not have that maneuverability. Minimal line sets also make navigating heavy boat traffic much easier.

When fishing for spawning bound kings, let the fish dictate your line setups. Fall kings get into a pattern, and typically, the same lures run the same way will work for an entire season. See Chapter 14, for a complete discussion on how to catch spawning bound kings.

HOW TO CHOOSE THE RIGHT LURES WHEN OPTIONS ARE LIMITED

Solo anglers have great control over their group dynamic. Since you are limited in lines, it is easy to keep track of the lures and colors you have tried on a particular day. If action is slow, designate one line as an experimental rod. Every 10 to 15 minutes, change the lure, color or size.

Organize your lures before you go fishing. Keep a hot box with your favorite baits for each season. Develop a system where you can store spoons by size, brand or color—whatever works best for you. Keep your flies in a separate box as well. I organize my flies by size and color. Crank baits, dodgers and flashers should be organized so you don't spend time looking for lures when you are on the water.

When building a productive group dynamic, experiment with the ratio of clean lines to lines with attractors. One day you may find that one rod with a dodger and two clean spoons is the perfect spread. Another day, a pair of flashers with a lone spoon below may be the winning combo. Use your three lines to systematically build group dynamics and track what works. A small notepad on the dash will let you keep notes to reference what is working and what is not.

Doc Rupprecht and Jim Flickinger should be an inspiration to all of us. I learned many things about Great Lakes salmon and trout fishing from Doc. They were never fancy or elaborate in their techniques, but you would rarely out fish them. If you pick your days, you can tap into some great chinook fishing during much of the season. Remember, much of the success trolling for kings is dependent on your ability to duplicate or repeat the set ups that are producing fish. You have to pay attention to small details in order to repeat success. For most people, repeatability is easier when there is less going on!

CHAPTER 14

Advanced Shallow Water Tactics For Pre-Spawn Kings

You can almost feel the changes in the wind. It happens every year. The days grow shorter and Cub fans start talking about "next year," but you're spooling fresh line on reels and looking for your J-Plugs. You're still catching plenty of kings offshore but they begin to take on a different appearance. Once chrome sided, the big guys take on a bronze hue. Their skin toughens up, spot patterns darken across their backs and their jaws and teeth take on a ferocious look. It is only a matter of time. As the ninth inning of summer comes to a close, large, mature kings disappear from the deep, cold waters of the Great Lakes.

After spending their lives roaming deep, clear, open water terrorizing frantic schools of alewives, kings head for home. The monarchs of the Great Lakes make their final pilgrimage into shoreline shallows, rivers and harbors to continue their march with destiny.

To many salmon fanatics, autumn takes on an almost sacred meaning. Long boat rides, loads of electronics and mountains of deepwater trolling gear are not needed to catch pre-spawn kings as they swarm off river and harbor mouths. Each year thousands of people with limited Big Water experience have the opportunity to catch trophy chinook salmon close to shore.

The techniques used to catch kings once they arrive off river and harbor mouths are the simplest of the year. In fact, a minimal amount of tackle and electronics will get you started. The secret to success is to fish where kings are returning to spawn. That is 90 percent of the battle. For a complete discussion on locating fall kings, see Chapter 4.

KEYS TO EFFECTIVE TROLLING PATTERNS

On the fishology temperament scale, staging kings are moodier than at any other time in their lives. Have you ever been on the Atkins diet? Then, taken your spouse or children to an ice cream shop for dessert? You understand feeding related moodiness!

When targeting the shoreline your first order of business is to determine exactly *where* the fish are holding. Are fish spread along the shore for 2 miles on either side of the river? Or, are they tightly schooled in two or three spots a tenth of a mile from the pier heads? The schooling pattern of shoreline kings is important because it will dictate your trolling pattern. If the fish are spread out, then long passes will work. If the fish are tightly grouped, you will want to make tight passes, allowing you to spend maximum time with your lures in front of fish.

Your trolling pattern will determine the amount of lines you can run and how you deploy them. If you are making long passes along a beach, you can run multiple numbers of side planers. If you are making circular passes off pier heads, you will want to keep your lines to a minimum (riggers, Dipsies and a flat line) to reduce your turning radius.

When kings stack up in front of steams, rivers and harbors prior to moving upriver, they will congregate in tight groups. Therefore, much of the water off rivers and harbors will be void of fish. A few key areas will be loaded with big fish.

You need to figure out where the fish are holding. Then you must implement a trolling pattern that allows you to meticulously and repeatedly hit the strike zone. If you troll outside the fish by 20 feet, pre-spawn kings will not chase your baits down. You must pull your lures directly in front of staging kings. It's like hammering a nail. If you want to drive the nail into the wood, hit the head of the nail four times consecutively. But, if you hit the nail on every fifth swing of the hammer, it will take forever to build a house.

In the early stages of the run, kings fresh in from open water will spread out along the shoreline parallel to river and harbor mouths. These fish are *looking* for the stream, river or harbor they will ascend for spawning. As spawning approaches kings will move in and out from the shoreline. One day they may be 100 yards off the beach and two miles the next. Some kings will move into the shoreline at night, almost like a military reconnaissance mission. These fish will prowl the shallows and retreat to deeper water at sunrise. You can find these fish during the mid-day holding on drops and ledges in 30 to 60 feet of water.

The fall months give small boat anglers their best shot at catching trophy fish close to shore.

Eventually kings do locate their river or harbor of origin. Once they lock in on their natal stream, they become highly concentrated. As the run advances, fish will hold in the immediate surroundings (within a half mile) of river and harbor outlets. Kings will *stage* in these locations for a few days to a few weeks before swimming upriver to spawn.

Please understand that every region is different. The general patterns governing pre-spawn kings will be the same but kings will exhibit subtle behavioral differences from one river or harbor system to the next. When you fish different ports you will have to adapt your techniques and trolling patterns.

Remember, spawning kings are different animals than the fish you encountered offshore during the summer months. Their sole focus is reproduction. They are on a mission, and they are looking to move upstream. Their bodies have been genetically programmed to perpetuate the species. In their native West Coast environment, Pacific Kings migrate from the open ocean into rivers where some fish will migrate hundreds of miles inland to spawn. Great Lakes kings, however do not have to navigate as far inland to reach spawning reds.

The genetic factor naturally encrypted into salmon needs to be understood, as it has significant implications on your philosophy of presentation and lure selection. Kings undergo massive physiological changes during the spawning run. These changes impact the behavior of kings. Because of this, you are no longer trying to entice feeding fish into striking. Spawning bound kings are very territorial and aggressive. You should capitalize on this aggressive nature.

Your goal is to spend maximum time with your lures in front of kings. A large part of autumn success is based on patience. Some days, you may need to make a dozen passes through fish to trigger strikes. Many anglers make two or three passes and give up. Often it is just a matter of time. Yes, you may have a slow hour or two but if you work the

CURRENT FLOW + STRUCTURE = KINGS

fish and determine where they are holding and identify the lures they want, you will catch tons of fish. Patience is a virtue.

Once you isolate exactly where kings are holding, make passes over the fish from multiple angles or directions. If you find a directional and speed pattern that is working, keep hammering the nail on the head.

Coping with Boat Traffic

Boat traffic can be a negative factor. If traffic is heavy, you may be limited in where and how you troll. Every time I fish off a river or harbor mouth, I am amazed at the lack of respect anglers and boaters show one another. Some days you'd think some people left their brains in the glove compartment of their cars. If everyone works together and uses common sense, it is a much more enjoyable experience for all, except the fish, of course.

Common sense is imperative! Before turning, look around 360-degrees and make sure you have room to complete your turn without cutting someone off. Never troll on top of another boat. You both lose. Try to determine if the boats have a flow pattern. For example, off the Pike Creek in Kenosha, the boats will usually follow a general pattern where north bound boats take the inside (beach) and south bound boats stay to the outside in deeper water. This eliminates tension and confrontations. It only takes one boat to ruin the pattern. Also, monitor what other anglers are doing. If someone is hooked up with a running fish, turn out and give them room to fight the fish. If the fish are thick off a river mouth, but heavy boat traffic has pounded the area, look to the edges of the pack or secondary structure features just outside the river mouth. Kings will often drift out to these outer areas to escape traffic. Also, if a river mouth is crowded, return to the area after the crowds have left. Once kings get their nose into the river mouth, they don't leave.

Time of Day

Does time of day influence success for shoreline kings? I don't know why so many people are afraid to fish for kings in the middle of the day! Yes, the early morning and evening are prime times for kings, but it is also prime time for anglers! You will have maximum competition from other anglers during these peak periods. This leads to maximum pressure on the fish. If you go to a birthday party and there are 20 people, chances are, you will have a small piece of cake. If you go to the same party and only 2 people show up, your piece of cake will be much larger.

Late morning and early afternoon can produce excellent action simply because there are minimal boats working the fish. I have started many afternoon charters at 12:00 or 1:00 p.m. on bright sunny days and had tremendous action for kings along the shoreline. Part of that success was due to the fact that I had the fish to myself.

Lure selection for fall kings is heavily dependant on the hour of the day and light penetrations. If you are fishing in murky river run-off after a rain, stained river water will darken shoreline water to the point that kings cannot see your lures. Bright sunlight will penetrate this murky water and allow kings to see your lures in the dirty water. Copper and orange are two of the best colors to use in this condition. Under this scenario, you will not catch many fish early and late in the day, but you will crush the fish during the bright hours. Kings are also patternistic. Some years they will get into a groove of either a strong morning bite, or a strong afternoon bite.

THE INFLUENCE OF WATER TEMPERATURE ON PRE-SPAWN KINGS

Water temperature is far less of a factor influencing pre-spawn kings (compared to summer) but it still influences fish movements and has an impact on fishing success. When the internal biological clock sounds, kings will move into the shoreline regardless of external conditions. High water temperatures will not stop the shoreward migration. When the urge hits, pre-spawn kings will swim through warm water to locate their natal river.

While warm water won't stop kings from moving into the shore, it will minimize their activity. When water temperatures are above 68 degrees, shoreline kings are difficult to catch. When water temperature is between 63 and 68 degrees, pre-spawn kings will be sluggish but catchable. When the water drops below 63 degrees, kings become active and aggressive. Good results are possible in 55 to 62-degree water. Peak action for pre-spawn kings occurs when water is in the 44 to 54-degree range.

Regardless of water temperature, some kings will begin moving into river and harbor mouths during mid to late August. Even if the water is a balmy 65 to 70 degrees. Other kings will hang off the shoreline in 30 to 70 feet of water waiting for cooler water.

Sudden changes in water temperature will influence activity. A common occurrence during late August (in some regions) is a sudden turnover or upwelling of cold water along the shoreline. When this happens, the water will drop from the high 60's down into the 50 or 40-degree ranges. These cool downs will pull massive waves of kings into the shallows. When kings hit the shore in cold water, the action can be explosive as these are high-octane fish on the move. These early run fish are cruising the shoreline, looking for home. Cold water energizes fish making them much easier to catch.

Once the fish become acclimated to the river and harbor mouths, an onshore wind will frequently warm the waters back up. Kings will stay in the shallow water but they will often become very sluggish and more difficult to catch.

TECHNIQUES FOR PRE-SPAWN KINGS

You will find shoreline kings from the surface to the bottom. Whether the water is ice cold or warm, pre-spawn kings tend to move up and down in the their shoreline environment. The question you need to determine is, "Will I catch more kings on the surface, or near the bottom?" Pre-spawn kings behave differently from one region to the next. You will need to determine the ideal combination of side planers, downriggers, Dipsies and flat lines to produce fish. For example, Kenosha and Racine, Wisconsin, are less than 10 miles apart. Both ports host excellent runs of fall kings. When I fish off Kenosha, most of my shoreline kings will come off side planers. Off Racine, downriggers and Dipsies will produce most of my fish.

Just like chasing kings across open water, trolling speed is always an issue. Savvy anglers know that if fish are present but action is slow, trolling speed may be the issue. After setting lines and identifying my trolling pattern, I start going up and down with trolling speed. Many days, the sudden increases will trigger moody fall kings into striking. Neutral drops with large wobbling cranks will pause a bait long enough to draw a strike. It's the oldest trick in the book, but it continues to work.

Surface Tactics

Two methods of presenting surface lines for kings are available. The old fashioned flat line produces loads of kings every fall. Simply take a crank bait, such as a J-Plug or Rapala Husky Jerk, and let it back 75 to 200 feet behind the boat. No weight is needed. I run the flat line on either 17 lb. test mono or on 20 lb. test Fire Line. If using a super line, I attach a six-foot leader of 20 to 30 lb. test mono. My favorite flat line bait is a white gold number 5 J-Plug with a red ladder back. It doesn't get any simpler.

Inline planer boards are your second option. Yellow Birds are my favorite side planer for fall kings. They are easy to use and very efficient. When kings are cruising the beach in 3 to 10 feet of water, there is nothing better than a Yellow Bird to take a crank bait or spoon off to the side. Body baits are the favored baits off side planers. On some days, clean spoons will draw strikes. If cranks are not producing and kings are present, I will put a magnum spoon such as a Silver Streak on an outside planer. Like a change up pitch, this can trigger strikes when cranks fail.

Side planer set-ups are simple. If you are using plugs, you don't need any weight in front of the plug, but you need something to stop the board from sliding down and hitting the fish in the head. I use a 1/8-ounce keel sinker to stop the planer. For J-Plugs I like a 20 to 30 lb. test mono leader. For jointed minnows like Fastracs, Rapalas and Shad Raps I like a 17 lb. test leader off the keel sinker.

Set the bait back anywhere from 8 to 50 feet behind the planer. Lead distance off the planer is important, but will vary from one day to the next. For most of my shoreline kings, a 10 to 25-foot lead produces best. If kings are rolling but not striking, try running a J-Plug 10 to 15 feet off a board. This will hold it close to the surface. One to four planers can be deployed per side, depending on traffic, seas and number of people on board. When running multiple side planers, run the outside planer longest. I like to choke the inside planer as this will minimize tangles when a big king hits a Dipsy and runs to the side.

Stream and river mouths are dynamite places to troll after a rain. When trolling off creek mouths, I like to put the boat in 6 to 12 feet of water and run side planers up over wave troughs right along the beach.

When targeting murky river run-off, bright sunlight will allow kings to see your lures.

When kings cruise the beach, planers *kicking sand* are studs. I like to pull the planers past the mouth of the outflow. Watch what direction the river outflow moves along the beach. Kings will stack up in the river runoff in the Lake. The color line where river water and Lake water meet is highly productive. Often, the river water, which is warmer than the Lake water, will remain on the surface. When this happens, the water beneath will be clear and you get a shade effect from above. Kings are light sensitive and will hold beneath the darker water.

While a number of crank baits are available, number 4 and 5 J-Plugs and J2000 jointed Rebel

Fastracs are the two most productive. Other good fall plugs include jointed Rapalas, Rapala Husky Jerks, Bomber Long A's, Shad Raps, Thunder Stiks, Rattle Traps, deep diving Rebels and Flat Fish. Hot colors change from year to year but all silver, all gold, pearl, copper, red top/gold belly and green/yellow belly are traditional favorites. There will be days when a pearl/blue/pink with black spot J-Plug will out fish all other colors. The magnum Green Alewife Silver Streak is a sleeper bait off outside Yellow Birds. When fishing in muddy or stained water, gold and copper are hot colors. The gold I prefer is called a *white gold*. It is not a bright gold, but appears slightly *darker* than silver. At times ladder-back patterns on plugs will increase their productivity.

Dipsy Divers

Kings love Dipsies, even in shallow water! When chasing pre-spawn kings in shallow water you can run divers on mono or super line. Super line will minimize break offs and save tackle. You will have to run them a little differently than when you were using them to reach deep layers of the water column.

Green, orange and clear size 1 divers, without rings, are preferred. The smaller O size Dipsy should also be considered. The smaller diver moves through the water differently than the size 1. This results in a different action being imparted to the trailing lure. This slight difference in presentation may trigger strikes. Since you are not trying to reach great depths, set the diver on a 2½ or 3-setting. This will keep the diver out to the side.

How far out you let the Dipsy will depend on the fish. There will be days when the fish will want the diver just below the surface and other days, you will need to set it to run closer to the bottom. Even if you are trolling in 6 to 12 feet of water, put a Dipsy in the water, as some kings will always strike Dipsy baits. In super shallow water run the diver out on 14 to 20 feet of line. The strikes on these rods will scare the daylights out of you! Some anglers will run two Dipsies per side in shallow water but most days one diver a side will work better.

Both spoons and plugs work on Dipsies. Leader test for both should be 20 lb. test. When running spoons on divers I prefer magnum spoons. In shallow water you do not need a dodger or flasher. Favorite Dipsy spoons include Silver Streaks, Fishlanders, Dreamweavers and Diamond Kings. When using cranks on divers the old fashioned number 4 J-Plug is hard to beat. Occasionally the number 3 size gets the nod. A wide variety of spoon colors can be used. I prefer glow spoons in shades of green, yellow, red and white, on divers. Other good colors are gold, gold/red, green, Green Dolphin, and the Caramel Dolphin.

Lure Color Selection

Let's take a detour and examine lure colors for fall kings. Remember, the trigger mechanism for staging kings is different than feeding kings. Pre-spawn kings are no longer actively feeding. Now, you are appealing to their aggressive nature. As spawning approaches kings become very territorial as they are jockeying for position, so to speak. Am I suggesting

The trigger mechanism of staging kings is very different from summer fish that are actively feeding.

kings have an ego? It sounds like it, doesn't it? The point being, you need to choose lures that agitate fish.

Pre-spawn kings can be very, very color selective, much like open water steelhead. I believe this is due to their territorial nature prior to spawning. They are moody and aggressive. What triggers their aggressive nature will change from hour to hour. Patterns may set up, but a degree of unpredictability will often prevail. For this reason, I change lure colors more often when fishing in shallow water than deep water.

If kings are rolling and marking on the graph, but strikes are few, keep working the fish. As you make continual passes over the fish, systematically designate several rods as change agents. You will change lure colors on these rods and try to isolate a pattern for the day. If you find that the fish want gold, then load up on gold. The best shoreline chinook anglers will often return to the dock with the same color lure on every rod after a successful trip. Let the fish tell you what color they want, and then give them plenty of that color to choose from.

Downriggers

I run plugs or spoons off riggers, depending on water depth. If I am trolling the beach in 5 to 12 feet, I may elect to only run side planers, Dipsies and a flat line. In this scenario, riggers will only get in the way as a hooked fish may dive down and tangle the rigger line. If I am fishing in 12 to 30 feet, two to four downriggers will be deployed. If the water is clear, I will use two riggers. In murky river runoff, four riggers.

When trolling off a river mouth, trace one rigger with a clean spoon or jointed J1000 Rebel along bottom contours. Kings love to sit along drop-offs and some days keeping a rigger within five feet of those drops will draw strikes. When following bottom contours in shallow water, you must constantly check lines to make sure weeds or zebra mussels do not foul baits. This is especially true when running a diving plug back 20 to 40 feet.

Lead length will be determined by boat traffic, water depth, water clarity and fish temperament. Early and late in the day, leads of 15 to 30 feet are ideal. As the sun climbs, lengthen your leads. If you are trolling in murky river runoff, then shorter leads of 20 to 40 feet will produce during the mid-day. If kings are spread out along the shore and the water is clear, then you will need to stretch baits back 60 to 100 feet off riggers. Sometimes I will only run two riggers with long leads in shallow, clear water. Since you are fishing in less than 30 feet of water, you do not need heavy downrigger weights.

My lure selection off riggers is basic and timeless. Jointed J2000 Rebel Minnows have been historical studs. They can be run in 25 feet of water or 8 feet of water. They have great action but do not dive to deep, reducing the amount of hitchhikers (zebra mussels). Favorite colors for the Rebels include black/silver, black/gold and orange/gold. J-Plugs and Grizzlies also produce plenty of fish off riggers, especially when working deeper harbor and river mouths. If you can troll at speeds of less than 1.5 kts, then M2 Flat Fish should also be considered. Flat Fish will spin and tangle lines if you go much faster than 1.5 Kts. If you want to use spoons, the same baits you used during the summer months will produce in the fall.

CASTING FOR SHALLOW WATER GIANTS

When I was younger, I was much more adventurous. As soon as my friends and I gained our driving privileges, every free moment was spent chasing autumn kings. We would frequently drift local harbors casting crank baits for kings. When I entered the charter trade I even ran charters where we would use spinning gear and cast plugs and spoons for kings.

I'll never forget one early charter experience on my first charter boat, a 23-foot inboard Mako, the *Rainmaker II*. After introductions I informed my clients that we would be casting large plugs on spinning rods to large king salmon. Upon arriving at our destination everyone was quite eager to begin fishing as large kings were rolling all around the boat. As I passed out spinning rods I quickly explained the routine to my clients who were spread out around the boat. I was on the bow giving a casting 101 tutorial to one person when an excited voice from the stern cried out, "How long do you let the fish have it before setting the hook?" I turned around and to my amazement the gentleman had opened the bale of the spinning reel and line was flying off the bail! This angler had felt the strike and thought you needed to free-spool line first! We boated that fish and I learned the value of spelling out instructions.

Can you catch kings casting? Absolutely. Can you catch more casting than trolling? Some days, yes. My point being, casting for spawning bound kings is a viable option. Casting is a presentation that is ideally suited for small and mid-size boats. It is a different way of fishing that many anglers enjoy. Casting gives you great control as you can stay on top of active fish. The key, therefore, is to identify where kings are holding and then set up a drift across the fish. It's really no different than drifting a flat in Florida.

Spinning or bait casting gear will work. Super line as well as mono can be used. I like light equipment so I would go with 8 to 12 lb. test mono line on a medium light-spinning rig. Plugs such as Fastracs and M2 Flat Fish will produce all the kings you can handle. If it is windy, spoons will cast easier than plugs. You may also want to try tube jigs or soft plastics such as a jig and twister tail. The same colors you use for trolling will work for casting.

You can never start a child fishing too early!

Fall fishing is an ideal time for anglers with limited big water experience. The fish are easy to locate, and you don't need a lot of extra equipment to catch them. If you are new to Great Lakes chinook fishing, autumn is a great time to begin your journey!

Fishermen are unique. They are highly stimulated by the crisp air of an early morning, first light reflecting off the water, the anticipation of the strike, the sound of a *screaming* drag and the sight of a trophy king salmon cutting the water like a shark. Whether your passion is pulling bass out of the stumps, chasing salmon across open water or casting handcrafted flies into a mountain stream, you have a magical spot that resonates deep in your heart.

The magnetic draw of fishing reaches deep into the heart of a fisherman. Much like an emotion, it penetrates every ounce of your being. The passion of fishing frequently begins early in life and is nurtured by sunrises, summer storms and photographs of trophy fish. For many, it becomes an obsession. Like an appetite, it is powerful, and if given the chance, can consume you. It finds its deepest expression and fulfillment when you are on the water.

I was drawn to fishing like little boys are drawn to puddles. When I was a young child, my family would make a trip each summer to central Iowa. You need to understand, to a six-year old boy, the fields and rivers of central Iowa were Paradise and Disney World rolled into one great place! It was on those early vacations that Granddad took me fishing. Granddad, who was always full of stories, would pack my sisters, cousins and I into his car and we'd head down to the Skunk, Raccoon or Des Moines rivers to fish for catfish, bullheads, sunfish, or anything with fins.

Young boys full of energy and imagination don't just go fishing, they go on adventures. Do you remember what it was like to be six years old? The imagination of a young boy is as large as the Western landscape and as creative as a first grade classroom. My early Hawkeye fishing trips were true adventures that typically began the night before. You see, Granddad believed the best fishing bait was a fat, juicy night crawler.

When I was growing up, you didn't go to a vending machine to buy bait. The best worm was a worm you pulled with your own hand from the earth.

Fishing is more than just the act of putting a line in the water. For a young child, looking for worms on a summer night or exploring the edge of a streambed is as entertaining as the fishing itself. For an adult, the gentle conversation that accompanies a fishing trip, rigging tackle the night before an outing or the journey to a favorite lake is frequently as memorable as the fishing itself.

Perhaps you were drawn to fishing at an early age. Maybe it was the first sight of a bobber dipping beneath the surface. Maybe it was that summer afternoon, toes dangling in the water, when an unknown tug on the end of the line pulled you out of a dream. But at some time, on some river, lake or ocean, something happened. Deep within your heart, something was triggered. Fishing was in your blood for life. Fishing, and the events surrounding fishing, pierced your soul. You drew pleasure from the extreme simplicity of the sport, found excitement in the pursuit of fish, fellowship on the journey, and refreshment at the source.

Fishing is a passion that tugs at your heart. From your earliest adventures to the local pond, your love of fishing grew. The need to wet a line is almost as important as the need for oxygen. If we go more than a few minutes without oxygen, we literally cease to be human. We die. For many, fishing, and the events surrounding a fishing adventure, breathes life into our minds, bodies and soul. Fishing inspires us and refreshes us. The journey of a fishing adventure leads you to a quiet place where you can catch your breath and reflect on life.

The need to wet a line is not as extreme as the body's need for oxygen. But the need to *nourish* the soul is vital. Fishermen understand passion because fishing is a sport that fosters passion in the heart. From the anticipation to the preparation to the journey to the catch and home again, the world surrounding fishing nurtures passion; and waters it with beauty, challenge, mystery and fellowship.

In this book, I've shared the secrets that I rely on to catch trophy king salmon for a living. While these tactics and secrets will help you catch more fish, I feel like I would be doing you a disservice if I fail to share one final tactic. This final tactic far surpasses the best day on the water, any tournament victory, or the biggest fish in the Lake. It is really the greatest secret in the world. It is a mystery, full of grace, but shrouded in simplicity. It is the foundation of my success and it has eternal power to expand your horizon beyond anything you can imagine.

Have you ever been fishing when a fog bank closed in around you? Without your electronics and a compass, it's easy to lose your bearings. A heavy fog is suffocating and cuts you off from the real world. Fog reduces your visibility, it obscures reality, and leads to confusion. There was a time in my life when I was lost in a fog bank of anger, depression, alcohol, women and drugs. But, by the grace of God, I was rescued from the fog. I became a new man through the blood of Jesus Christ. The aches, frustrations, and disappointments of a life chasing illusions melted away and I was confronted with the Truth. The anger and depression no longer tormented me. Through Christ, I had the power to defeat the vices that were consuming me.

Be honest for a moment. You may think you're in control, but today may be the day you are diagnosed with cancer, your child may be the victim of a tragic and unexpected accident or a Global Entity may politely tell you, "you are no longer needed." What do you really control? Let's be honest, the real question is, *what are you giving up control to?* If you think you have all the answers, then you should follow the advice of an American landmark, a major brewery, and *"go for the gusto, make it a good one!"* Because one day, your world, your life will end.

You know friend, Jesus Christ made a bold statement when He claimed to be the Son of God. Do you understand this? Either He is the Son of God or he is a raving lunatic. Who is Jesus Christ to you? The Son of God or a lunatic? One day you will be faced with this decision and your choice will echo throughout eternity. If you want to taste true freedom then look beyond the gunnels of your boat to the Gospel. What is the Gospel?

The message of the Gospel is really about passion. The Gospel is the epicenter of God's love for his people. It is the adventure of the One True God, who *so loved the world* that he left his Celestial dwelling and walked with us, fished with us, broke bread with humanity, wept with us, and then . . . he died for us. He did all this, and so much more, for you and for me. John 3:16 is the heart of the Gospel Message, "For God so loved the world that he gave his one and only Son, that whoever believes in him shall not perish but have eternal life." As a child, you may have heard John 3:16. But what does it really mean? Is John 3:16 a distant memory or does it speak into your life today?

To fully appreciate this verse, you need to look to Jesus Christ. The Gospel tells us that Jesus Christ is passionate! He so passionately loved the world that he was willing to go to the Cross and die for *you* and for me. You are the recipient of God's passion! How does that make you feel? The God that formed the Rocky Mountains, carved the Grand Canyon, and painted the spots on an autumn Brook Trout is passionately in love with you! The Gospel message is Good News!

The Cross is the intersection of God and humanity. It is at the Cross where Christ took the place of the lost and paid a debt that no mortal man, woman or child could pay. Jesus died on a cross, but he was not held captive by death for He defeated death. The Bible tells us that Jesus rose on the third day and the risen Lord appeared to Mary, Martha, the Disciples, and over 500 witnesses! Bottom line, people, the Gospel is eternal and your understanding of John 3:16 has eternal consequences.

There was a time in my life where catching the *most* and *biggest* fish every day was the driving force in my life. I had run thousands of charters, been caught in countless fog banks, hammered by storms and heavy seas, and caught more fish than most mortals dream of—but I was lost. From an eternal perspective my life was bankrupt. My internal compass was calibrated on lesser things and ultimately my life was empty. When I surrendered my life to Christ, I was a new creation. With Christ, I tasted true freedom and my horizon was washed by grace.

If you stand at the water's edge on a calm day and listen, you can't deny it. There is a natural rhythm built into the waters that sustain our planet. What about you? What sustains you? How do you navigate from one foggy, damp Monday morning to the next? What rhythm does your heartbeat follow? Is the pace of your life set by the standards of this world? Or is your life calibrated to a higher standard?

What is the orientation of *your* life? I challenge you this day to look beyond yourself. The Gospel is a message of grace that calls you to calibrate your heart, the compass of your soul, to the heart of Jesus Christ. It is a free gift, given by an eternal God who calls you by name.

The Gospel calls for a response. It calls you to live a life in relationship with Jesus Christ. I challenge you to drink deeply from the well of life. If you are living without Christ, you are like a man standing with one foot on a wharf and the other foot on a boat pulling away. You will be torn in two. A life without Christ is empty and ultimately bankrupt.

The greatest secret I can share with you is the eternal love of Christ. To learn more about having a relationship with Jesus Christ, visit *www.allaboutgod.com,* or let me send you a free book. You can email me at *captaindan@bluehorizonsportfishing.net* or call 877.783.2270.

More Ways To Increase Your Enjoyment On The Water!

◆ On the water fishing class is in session May-October! Book an instructional fishing charter with Captain Dan Keating onboard the *BLUE HORIZON* and receive one-on-one instructions. Learn how to target kings with light line, use wire divers for deep water action, group dynamic fundamentals or how to finesse spawning kings from the shoreline. Classes are custom tailored to your needs—you tell us what you want to learn! To book a charter email: *captaindan@bluehorizonsport fishing.net* or phone 847.395.5730.

◆ Order Dan's first book, *Great Lakes Salmon And Trout Fishing, The Complete Troller's Guide.* $24.95 plus $4.00 shipping and handling. (Illinois residents add $1.62 sales tax)

◆ Help your friends catch more fish! Send them a copy of *Keating on Kings: Great Lakes Chinook Tactics Way Beyond The Basics.* $24.95 plus $4.00 shipping and handling. (Illinois residents add $1.62 sales tax)

◆ Attend a highly informative fishing seminar given by Captain Dan Keating. Dan speaks at fishing clubs and Sport Shows across the Great Lakes. To have Dan speak at your club or for his speaking schedule call 877.783.2270 or email *captaindan@bluehorizonsportfishing.net.*

◆ Look for our upcoming video series and future books!

◆ Visit *www.bluehorizonsportfishing.net* for more information.